MOTOR ACTIVITIES FOR THE UNDERACHIEVER

MOTOR ACTIVITIES FOR THE UNDERACHIEVER

By

DAVID B. NICHOLS, Ed.M.

DARYL R. ARSENAULT, Ed.M.

DONNA L. GIUFFRE, B.S.

Photographs by

Walter J. Rossini

Drawings by

Paul A. Nichols

CHARLES   C   THOMAS   •   PUBLISHER
Springfield   •   Illinois   •   U.S.A.

Published and Distributed Throughout the World by
CHARLES C THOMAS • PUBLISHER
Bannerstone House
301-327 East Lawrence Avenue, Springfield, Illinois, U.S.A.

With THOMAS BOOKS *careful attention is given to all details of
manufacturing and design. It is the Publisher's desire to present books that
are satisfactory as to their physical qualities and artistic possibilities and
appropriate for their particular use.* THOMAS BOOKS *will be true to those
laws of quality that assure a good name and good will.*

Printed in the United States of America
V-R-1

Library of Congress Cataloging in Publication Data

Nichols, David B
    Motor activities for the underachiever.

    Bibliography: p.
    Includes index.
    1. Underachievers.   2. Slow learning children.
3. Motor learning.   I. Arsenault, Daryl R., joint
author.   II. Giuffre, Donna L., joint author.
III. Title.
LC4661.N52   371.92'6   80-13882
ISBN 0-398-04090-7

To Richard L. Swift
whose early vision and overwhelming concern
for helping children with special needs
has been an inspiration
for each of us.

INTRODUCTION

HAVE you ever witnessed the rejection felt by a child who was the last picked by two captains choosing teams for a simple schoolyard game? Have you ever seen the frustration in a little girl who didn't have the necessary balance skills to ride a bicycle, but all her friends did? Have you ever noted that the skilled athletes are constantly improving and being rewarded, while the less skilled withdraw from activity because of less satisfaction and limited opportunities to participate?

The ideas and programs in this book have grown out of a concern by physical education teachers for children who are being left out and emotionally hurt and are not progressing physically at the rate that they should. The information being shared is written for parents, teachers, and physical education professionals who care and are willing to do something for children who need help in reaching their maximum potential.

Every child is entitled to and needs a good physical education program. Learning basic motor skills and developing physical fitness during the primary years is essential in the normal development of a child. Muscular coordination creates a positive self-image in a child, while awkwardness and weakness can foster self-doubt and hamper the building of confidence. In a well planned physical education program, the average and above average student is able to develop the motor skills, body control, and muscular coordination necessary for normal motor development, but a more comprehensive program may be needed for some children. These children need a more individual and specialized program in addition to their weekly physical education program. Individualized instruction should be given to these children as early as possible in their development. The ultimate goal of an adaptive program is to provide successful experiences for children, to create a positive self-image, and to prepare each child for an enjoyable and active adulthood. It is our belief that individuals who feel good about themselves and who are actively able to participate in life are more at ease with their status in the world. Children who learn how to move and function, and know how to succeed rather than fail, will no longer withdraw from activity, but be the first to pursue challenging experiences.

ACKNOWLEDGMENTS

W E would like to gratefully acknowledge the support given by John Gleason, Walter Marcille, Louise Rozzi, Richard Valle, David Silva, Arthur Iworsley, Dorothy Christopher, and David Huston whose humor kept us going. With special thanks to Pamela Kvilekval and the Andover Public School children.

D.B.N.
D.R.A.
D.L.G.

CONTENTS

MOTOR ACTIVITIES FOR THE UNDERACHIEVER

Chapter 1

TEACHER AND TEACHING METHODS

TEACHER

O UR interpretation of an adaptive physical education program may differ from other professionals' views. Many professionals have defined adaptive physical education as "correctives" or "remedial" and have looked at the field as medically oriented. However, physical therapists working with the schools have taken over the therapy aspects of adaptives and have given the adaptive physical education specialist the opportunity to concentrate on developing basic motor skills and physical fitness in the weak and overweight students, and to work more closely with the physical education teacher. The adaptive physical education specialist should possess a well-rounded physical education background with an emphasis in child development. As a specialist, the teacher should be sensitive to the child's personal needs and individual differences. The adaptive physical education teacher who can work with children in small groups or individually, is the ideal instructor for the child with motor development weaknesses.

In many cases, school systems are unable to employ a full-time adaptive physical education specialist and must rely on the services of a regular physical education teacher. Physical education teachers who can set aside time in their daily schedule to work with a small number of children to carry out a motor development program can provide a tremendous service to those that they teach.

The teaching of children who demonstrate a weakness in the area of motor development may come from a wide variety of sources. Since children learn from a myriad of individuals and experiences, positive learning activities can benefit the child no matter who the teacher is. Any individual that can instill confidence, provide enjoyment, and increase motor skill level will be a valuable asset to a child with a weakness in motor activity. Classroom teachers who observe perceptual and gross-motor difficulties may use motor activities to reinforce skills in the classroom or on the playground. Nursery school teachers who are very much involved in the physical development of the young child can provide enjoyable movement experiences for their preschool children.

Since the child's first learning experiences derive from the imitation of family members, parents can serve as key instructors for the child. Older siblings who play with the child can generate enthusiasm for activity and provide enjoyable experiences for their younger brothers and sisters in their leisure time. By participating with the child in the activities in this book, specialists, teachers, parents, and friends can initiate activity designed to improve the child's development and increase his self-esteem.

TEACHING METHODS

The selection of appropriate learning progressions and challenging activities are of the utmost importance in improving a child's physical fitness or skill level. Many who have motor development weaknesses have omitted necessary steps in the normal physical progressions from one movement to the learning of another. For example, a child who has not developed certain skills related to striking would find it extremely difficult to hit a baseball with a bat 2 inches in diameter. The adaptive specialist, through his assessments, must discover where each student's level of ability lies and provide success-oriented and challenging activities that fit the needs of the child. A young child may begin to learn striking skills by hitting a balloon with his hand and later with an oversized table tennis paddle. The child could then progress to the more complex skills of striking a suspendable ball with the hand or paddle, or hitting a plastic ball placed on a batting tee with an oversized bat. A child with weak stomach muscles who is unable to complete a single sit-up may begin strengthening those muscles by throwing the arms forward as the sit-up is started or by using an incline board as an aid in completing the exercise.

There is no limit to what can be physically achieved if the proper progressions are coupled with the student's desire to improve.

When explaining an activity, the instructor should make sure the objectives are understood by the child. Various approaches should be taken in teaching skills since children differ in learning styles. A movement exploration or *problem-solving* approach may be appropriate for certain activities and specific children, while others may need a traditional *demonstration-style* approach. While some children learn best in partner activities or in a group setting, other children may need *one-to-one* teacher direction. Each child will have his own style of learning and it is up to the teacher to determine the most effective teaching approach.

One very effective teaching method in the motor development program involves the use of *activity stations*, which children use either individually or with partners on a rotation system (fig. 1). If a specific motor area is being focused on, such as balance, stations involving balance activities should be set up. Activities such as stilt walking, trampoline bouncing, bal-

Figure 1. Working in "Stations."

ance beam walking, and scooter riding would be arranged in areas for students to use to improve their dynamic balance. Students should spend a certain amount of time at each activity and, on a signal by the teacher, rotate to another station. The students know which station to go to by moving in a certain pattern or by following a coding system using numbers, shapes, or colors. This teaching method allows the teacher to work with specific children on problem areas while the rest of the class is still actively participating in a learning experience.

At times it may be advantageous for the teacher to use stations that teach a variety of skills. The teacher can design stations for specific needs. Activities involving eye-hand coordination, locomotor movement, balance, and spatial awareness can be set up in different areas. A child with weakness in locomotor skills could stay at that station for a longer period of time before rotating to the next.

There are numerous activities and effective methods that help children to improve physical fitness levels. Progressive resistance exercise, circuit training, fitness games, calisthenics, isometric exercise, obstacle courses, flexibility exercises, and interval training are effective techniques for aiding children. A class in physical fitness training would incorporate many of these approaches to reach each child.

A typical physical fitness class would begin with an ample warm-up period that would include flexibility exercises. The warm-up would be sustained long enough to increase muscle temperature, blood circulation rate, and oxygen transportation. Since flexibility is related to habitual movement patterns for each person and each joint, stretching exercises would be included. Fitness charts that tell the student which resistance exercise should be performed, along with the number of sets and repetitions of the exercise in the set, would be designed for each student prior to the class meeting.

After the warm-up, the student can read his individual chart, and by using either a station-to-station or a circuit training method, would begin the progressive resistance exercises. Even though the exercise stations would be the same, they can be individualized for each student by altering the amount of repetitions or the way the exercise is carried out, depending on ability. At a chin-up station, one student may work on increasing the total number of pull-ups he can complete while another is encouraged to break his own personal record in certain exercises or even try to break the class record.

After completing the resistance exercises, the student would work on improving endurance through distance running or interval training. Homogeneous running groups would run short distances a number of times or try to increase their longer running distances.

Motivational Techniques

Many of the students you will be working with will enjoy the program and activities you offer without any special motivational techniques. Some students are highly motivated intrinsically, while others may have no self-motivation and need to be stimulated in some way. Success is the key word. To some degree, each of these students has experienced failure in physical activities and needs to feel some success to develop a positive attitude toward activity.

Successful experiences can be established if skills are taught in progressions and if the student can complete the task he is attempting. Children need to know their level of ability and the progression they are working towards.

Students will be more willing to complete tasks if a reward is involved. Different types of reinforcers can be used to gain the appropriate responses from the student. Positive verbal reinforcement is usually a sufficient reward when a desired task is completed by the student. A positive reaction by the teacher can be very rewarding for most children and will increase the chances that the desired behavior will occur again.

Some students may require a tangible reward. Contingency contracting may be necessary in these cases. A verbal agreement between you and the student will specify what tasks must be accomplished before a reward is given. The reward should be something meaningful to the child so that he will be willing to work for it. For example, if the student completes stations one, two, three, and four, he may have five minutes of free time at the end of class.

Other tangible rewards you may use are personal progress charts or progress certificates. When the student can actually see his progress, this can be very stimulating. Personal progress charts are a means of showing individual accomplishments. To see a score of twenty sit-ups increase to thirty sit-ups on a chart can visually show success to the student. A progress certificate can be given to a student when he reaches certain goals in his program. Examples of these types of certificates can be found in Appendix C.

Stimulating environments can be motivating in themselves. Brightly colored targets, new types of equipment, and non-competitive games can create a "fun" atmosphere for the child. He may be more willing to try new activities and learn to enjoy participation.

Your students need to be assessed individually to see how they will need to be motivated and what type of technique will be appropriate to their needs. Always remember that the teacher is the key to the students' success.

Chapter 2

SCREENING AND SCHEDULING

SCREENING

EVEN the non-professional is able to observe and identify children with serious coordination problems, but subjective screening cannot surpass objective testing to pinpoint weaknesses.

There are many drawbacks in the testing devices that are offered in the areas of motor development and physical fitness for children. Many do not relate directly with physical education and are geared more towards fine-motor abilities, some are very diagnostic and take too long to administer, and others are designed for the wrong age group or population.

Screening a total school population can be a tedious undertaking and many school systems have shied away from screening because of the paper work and time involved and because there is no hope of the results being used to initiate a special program. Screening and the identification of children, however, is necessary to substantiate the need for such a program.

Before selecting a screening device that will fit your needs, you should ask the following questions: How much time can you devote to screening? Who will be your target population? Will the screening results help in initiating a program?

There are many tests available dealing with perceptual-motor abilities. The one you choose will depend on your needs and the age group you wish to administer it to. Most tests have been designed to be given individually and may be useful in screening referrals rather than a total population. Some of these include the following:

AYRES Southern California Perceptual-Motor Tests

Ayres, Jean A. Southern California Perceptual-Motor Tests.

Los Angeles, California: Western Psychological Services, 1969.
Target population:
normal children ages four to eight
Test components:

1. Imitation of postures
2. Crossing the midline of the body
3. Bilateral motor coordination
4. Right-left discrimination
5. Static balance eyes open
6. Static balance eyes closed

Cratty Six-Category Gross Motor Test

Cratty, Bryant, J. Motor Activity and the Education of Retardates.
Philadelphia: Lea and Febiger, 1969.
Target population:
normal children, ages four to eleven
educable retarded, ages five to twenty
trainable retarded, ages five to twenty-four
Test components:

1. Body perception
2. Gross agility (rise to a stand)
3. Static balance
4. Locomotor agility
5. Ball throwing
6. Ball tracking

Frostig Movement Skills Test Battery

Orpet, R. E. Frostig Movement Skills Test Battery. Palo Alto,
California: Consulting Psychologists Press, Inc., 1972.
Target population:
children, ages six to twelve
Test components:

1. Bilateral eye-hand coordination
2. Unilateral coordination
3. Eye-hand and fine motor coordination

4. Visual-motor coordination involving aim and accuracy
5. Spine flexion
6. Leg strength
7. Running speed and agility
8. Gross agility
9. Abdominal strength
10. Dynamic balance
11. Static balance
12. Arm and shoulder girdle strength

Purdue Perceptual-Motor Survey

Roach, Eugene G., and Kephart, Newell C. The Perceptual-Motor Survey.
Columbus, Ohio: Charles E. Merrill Publishing Co., 1966.
Target population:
normal children, ages six to ten
Test components:

1. Balance and posture
2. Body image and differentiation
3. Perceptual-motor match (chalkboard activities)
4. Ocular control
5. Form perception

Move-Grow-Learn Movement Skills Survey

Orpet, R. E., and Heutis, T. L. Move-Grow-Learn Movement Skills Survey.
Chicago: Follett Publishing Co., 1971.
Target population:
normal children, ages eight and under
Test components:

1. Coordination and rhythm (gross-motor, fine-motor, eye-motor)
2. Agility
3. Flexibility
4. Strength
5. Speed

6. Balance (static, dynamic, object)
7. Endurance
8. Body awareness (laterality)

Andover Perceptual-Motor Test*

The Andover Perceptual-Motor Test developed in 1972, deals with basic perceptual-motor areas necessary for normal development and motor learning. The test was designed as a quick screening device and not as a diagnostic tool. The complete test can be given to a group of up to twenty-five students in two, thirty minute class periods.

Target population:
normal children, ages four to seven
Test components:

1. Balance — the ability to maintain body position and equilibrium both in movement and in stationary body positions.
2. Eye-hand coordination — the ability to coordinate the eyes and hands to accomplish a task.
3. Locomotion — the ability to ambulate the body through space. A combination of strength, coordination, and balance is needed to move the body from one position to another.
4. Spatial awareness — the ability to make spatial judgments and perceive the body in relation to other objects in space.
5. Rhythm — the ability to hear, interpret the sounds heard, and respond to that which is interpreted.

SCHEDULING

When the evaluation process is completed, the scheduling of students can begin. Ideally, students should be grouped homogeneously according to age, but sometimes this is impossible. Students with motor development weaknesses are usually best serviced in groups no larger than eight, while students in physical fitness training programs can be seen in groups as large as

---

*The complete test can be found in Appendix A.

twelve. If groups become too large, the amount of individual attention you can provide will be minimal and the progress may not be as rapid.

The idea behind having an adaptive physical education program is to provide these students with daily physical education, and this should be kept in mind when scheduling. The students should continue to participate in a regular physical education program, and the adaptive program should be a supplement to this.

In order to get the kind of schedule the student needs, there must be a close working relationship between the adaptive specialist, the principal, the classroom teacher, and other specialists. Many of the students you will want to schedule will also have problems in other areas such as reading and mathematics. This should be taken into consideration when selecting an appropriate time for service. In many situations you may need to use the time before school, during recess, or during specialists' time (music, art) to provide instruction.

Chapter 3

BODY IMAGE, LATERALITY,
SPATIAL AWARENESS

Figure 2. Imitating Letters.

BODY image is probably the most important area of motor development. This is the basis for all motor activity and an area that should be fully developed before attempting complex motor tasks. A child needs to know his body and how it moves in order to learn to perceive things in relation to himself. He needs to distinguish body parts and the different sides of his body. He also learns to use them independently and in unison with one another.

The following activities follow a sequence to build body image, develop laterality, and to improve the ability to make appropriate spatial judgments.

ACTIVITIES DEALING WITH BODY IMAGE

Identification of Body Parts

The child is asked to locate different body parts such as hand, head, and foot. These are more easily identified than specific parts such as joints (elbows, shoulders, and ankles).

Combining Parts

The child is asked to combine body parts on command. For example, "Put your elbow on your knee; put your thumb on your shoulder."

Body Tracing

Lay the child on a large sheet of paper and trace the outline of the child. As you trace, you may name parts as you draw around them. When completed, the child can color different body parts.

Body Image Twister

Using the same idea as the commercially sold game, you can make colored shapes to place on the floor in a group and corresponding smaller shapes for cards that give the child the directions. The teacher or another child can read the cards to the performer. For example, a red triangular shaped card picturing a head (fig. 3A) would mean that the performer should place his head on the red triangle on the floor (fig. 3B).

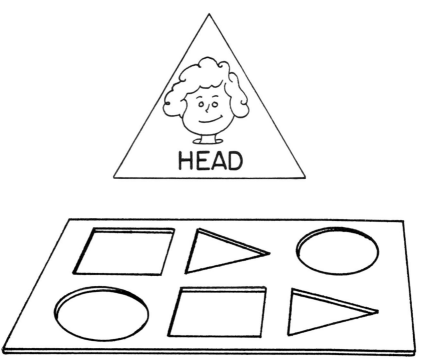

Figure 3. Body Image Twister.

Suspendable Ball With Parts

Using a suspendable ball, the child can strike the ball with different body parts. For example, "Strike the ball with your fist, your elbow, your forehead."

Balloon Image

Using a large round balloon, the child can attempt to keep it up in the air by using different body parts. The hand, thumb, pinkie, head, elbow, foot, fist, and wrist can be used.

Mirror Image

Using slow tempo music, position yourself in front of the child and begin to make slow movements for the child to imitate. He must be reminded that you are the "mover" and he is the "image" in the mirror that you are standing or sitting in front of.

Imitating Position

With your back to the child, perform arm and leg positions for the child to imitate (fig. 4).

Figure 4. Imitating Position.

Mechanical Man

The child lays on his back on the floor with arms and legs close to the body. On command, he slides his arms and legs open and closed. Different variations can be used to develop integration of the body. One side of the body is moved and then the other side. One arm is moved with the opposite leg and then the other arm with the opposite leg.

Body Surfaces

The child is asked to identify body planes. For example, "Touch the front of your body, your side, the top of your head, the bottom of your feet."

Body Surfaces and Objects

After demonstrating the ability to identify body surfaces, the child is asked to relate these surfaces to other objects in space. For example, "Lie on the mat on your side; touch the wall with your front; place your back against the chair."

Hoop Jumping

Hoops are placed on either side of a central line taped on the floor. As the child jumps into the hoop he must say whether he is jumping to the right or left of the line (fig. 5).

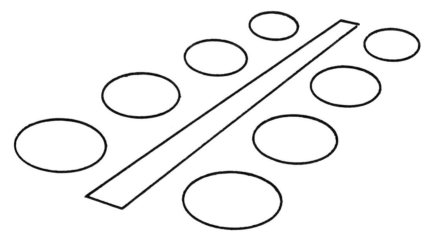

Figure 5. Hoop Jumping.

Playground Balls

Balls should be 6 to 8 inches in diameter. Each child should be reminded to keep his eyes on the ball. Drawing a face, name, or design on the ball with chalk or paint can aid the child in tracking.

1. The child holds the ball in front of the body, on the left side of the body, on the right side of the body, and in front of the stomach, back, knees, feet, and other body parts.
2. The child lifts the ball from the floor to knee level, waist level, shoulder level, and eye level.
3. The child rolls the ball up on the feet, ankles, shins, knees, thighs, waist, stomach, chest, shoulders, and head.
4. The child rolls the ball around his waist, thighs, knees, and ankles.

ACTIVITIES DEALING WITH LATERALITY

During the primary years, a sense of laterality or a feeling for a difference in the sides of the body begins to develop. You can help this development by incorporating laterality tasks in other activities the child may be asked to perform. For example, if the child is practicing walking the length of the beam, he can hold a bean bag in his right hand while he is walking. If the child is practicing ball handling skills, you can emphasize whether he is using his right or left hand. A piece of tape on the back of the hand can help to remind the child of his right as opposed to his left (fig. 6).

Figure 6. Tape Reminders.

Right/Left Line

Tape a line on the floor that changes direction every three or four feet (fig. 7). At each corner place a color as a signal for the child to stop walking. The child begins walking on the tape and as he reaches the color, he stops and indicates whether he will turn to the right or left to continue following the line.

Figure 7. Right/left Line.

Small Hand Apparatus

A balloon can be kept in the air by using either the right or the left hand. Other small hand apparatus such as a ball, hoop, or bean bag can also be used with one hand or the other.

Obstacle Course

A series of obstacles that the child must go through can help to develop serial memory and also force the child to make spatial judgments in relation to his own body. The child may be asked to crawl under a bench, roll on a mat, jump into a group of hoops, and walk through a horizontal ladder (fig. 8).

Figure 8. Obstacle Course.

ACTIVITIES DEALING WITH SPATIAL AWARENESS

Once the child has established a good body-image and internalized the concept of laterality, he needs to move in space with and without objects and obstacles. One way to improve spatial awareness is through a movement exploration approach. The child can learn to move in his own space and in a generalized space. He can learn to move while using small hand apparatus and learn to move with obstacles.

Red Rover

Children line up at one end of play area and the child who is "it" stands in the center. He dares the children to cross to the other side by challenging "Red Rover, Red Rover wants everyone with red on to cross over." The child crossing the area must determine a spatial plan and run to open areas where Red Rover cannot tag him.

Shipwreck

The instructor becomes the captain of the ship and commands the "mates" to different parts of the ship to perform different tasks. He may ask the children to run to the port side or skip to the stern. The child must make judgments as to where places are in relation to other places.

Total Body Movements

The child is asked to make different shapes with his body. Have him make a straight line, a curve, or a ball. If he recognizes letters, he may try to duplicate them using his body. For example, have the child make the letter "T," "L," "K."

Level Tag

Each child has a ball and on a signal from the instructor he has to tag other children at a level designated by the leader. The levels can be medium (between the shoulders and waist), high, or low. The children must tag the other children with their ball or they can block other balls with their own. When a child is tagged, he leaves the playing area.

Blind Man's Move

Children are blindfolded and positioned on a starting line. A leader asks the children to walk in different directions such as backward, forward, left or right. After a series of directions have been given, children remove their blindfolds and see who remains facing the leader. A new leader is chosen and the game continues.

Chapter 4

BALANCE

Figure 9. Dynamic Balance.

BALANCE is an individual's ability to maintain any body position against the force of gravity. This is an important motor area because it underlies more complex tasks such as throwing, kicking, hopping, etc. Balance can be broken down into three major areas: balance in a position (static balance), balance while in motion (dynamic balance), and recapturing balance upon landing from mid air.

The primary method of learning balance is through imbalance. Children placed in different balance positions and states of imbalance will have to compensate by adjusting their center of gravity to achieve equilibrium. By providing a series of activities that are progressively more difficult, the child's sense of balance will improve. The following balance activities are in sequence so that a child can add one success to another as each skill is built upon a previous skill. As each new skill is acquired, the child's ability and confidence in maintaining equilibrium and control over his body will improve.

ACTIVITIES DEALING WITH STATIC BALANCE

If a child's balance is very poor and he seems to have poor body control, it may be helpful to place the child in the correct body position when performing static balance tasks, so that he is able to "feel" the position kinesthetically.

Diver's Balance

The child lifts the weight of his body to the toes of both feet as he holds his arms straight out in front of him. The child remains in this position for ten seconds. He can try to bend at the waist while maintaining balance on the toes as a more difficult task.

Knee Balance

The child, in a kneeling position, attempts to balance on one knee while his arms are out to the side. This position is held for ten seconds and the other knee is then used (fig. 10).

Figure 10. Knee Balance.

Stork Stand

From a standing position, the child lifts one leg off the floor placing the lifted foot on the opposite knee. He attempts to hold this position for ten seconds while using the arms for balance. Repeat with the other foot (fig. 11).

Swan Stand

The child leans forward at the hips and lifts the right foot off the floor. While balancing on the left foot, the child lifts the right leg behind and as high as possible (fig. 12). Repeat on the other foot.

Figure 11. Stork Stand.

Figure 12. Swan Stand.

Figure 13. V-sit.

"T" Scales

The child performs a swan stand with the body in a horizontal line parallel to the floor, with one leg as the point of balance. While performing the scale, the child should place his hands in different positions such as on the head, hips, towards the floor, and in different directions.

V-sit

The child sits on the floor and lifts his arms and legs into the air while balancing on the buttocks. This position is held for ten seconds (fig. 13).

Balance Points

In a hands and knees position facing the floor, a hands and feet position facing the floor, or hands and feet position facing upward, the child is asked to hold high and straight the following parts:

1. Right arm
2. Left arm
3. Right leg
4. Left leg
5. Right arm and right leg
6. Left arm and left leg
7. Right arm and left leg
8. Left arm and right leg

Indian Squat

From a standing position, the child crosses his legs and sits down on the floor. By shifting the weight of the body forward and pushing upward, the child returns to a standing position.

Tripod or Elephant Stand

To form a base, the child kneels and places both hands, palms flat on the mat in front of him, about shoulder width apart. The child places the head, at hairline level, ahead of the palms. These three points of contact with the mat form a triangle. From the base, the child moves forward, placing the left knee on the back of the left elbow and the right knee on the back of the right elbow.

Headstand

From a tripod position, the child either brings both legs up simultaneously or swings an extended leg upward while a bent leg pushes slightly off the mat. The body weight will shift forward on to the triangular base. The instructor can aid the child by holding the ankles when the stunt is first learned.

ACTIVITIES DEALING WITH DYNAMIC BALANCE

When teaching dynamic balance, it is important to remember the role that vision plays in performing such tasks. A meaningful progression would involve imposing varying degrees of visual stress.

Paper Walk

The child stands on two pieces of paper (one foot on each). He then slides to the left and to the right while keeping his feet on the paper.

Rug Twister

The child places a rug sample (can be purchased at a low cost at a carpet store) so that rubber backing faces upward. He stands on the rug and twists back and forth to move around the floor.

Knee Walk

The child places an eight inch rubber playground ball between the knees and practices walking while squeezing the ball with the legs so that the ball does not drop.

Tape Line

The simplest balance beam is a chalk or tape line on the floor. Colored lines and ropes placed on the floor can prove to be challenging balance paths that change direction and shape. Objects can be placed along the paths to go over, as well as bridges to go under. Along the path the child may attempt the following:

1. Walk forward, backward, and sideways.
2. Walk while balancing a bean bag or book on the head.
3. Walk on the toes or the heels of the feet.
4. Run, hop, or skip in different directions.
5. Balance a bat or stick in the palm of the hand while walking.

Hoop Leap

Spread hoops or rug samples randomly or in a path across the floor approximately one yard from each other. The child leaps from hoop to hoop and maintains a one foot static balance in each hoop for five seconds.

Limbo

High jump standards are set up and each child attempts to go under the bar without touching the floor with anything but their feet. The bar is lowered each time the child makes a successful pass, until it becomes extremely difficult for the child to go below the bar without touching it or falling.

Hopping

Hopping is an appropriate dynamic activity that the child should attempt on both the right and left foot. Can you —

1. Hop over objects using your left foot and then your right?
2. Hop with the eyes closed?
3. Hop while holding on to different objects?
4. Hop on a trampoline (careful spotting necessary)?

5. Hop in and out of tires?

ACTIVITIES DEALING WITH RECAPTURING BALANCE

Any situation that involves air to ground movement requires some degree of strength and balance. The landing requires recapturing balance on the ground. The factors that affect the recapturing of balance are the height in the air, the posture of the body in the air, the landing base, and the posture of the body when landing.

Can you —

1. Jump off a low bench landing with your two feet close together and in a squat position?
2. Jump off a low bench landing with your two feet inside of a hoop?
3. Jump off a low bench landing with your two feet together on a mat and perform a forward roll?
4. Jump off a low bench landing inside a hoop and proceed to jump into other hoops placed in a pattern in hopscotch fashion?
5. Jump forward off a box or a chair and clap your hands above your head in midair?
6. Jump forward off a box or chair with one foot going forward and the other backward and land safely with your legs back together?
7. Hop off a low bench on one foot and land on that same foot? Try the other foot.
8. Jump forward off a low bench and make a half turn in midair landing facing the bench?
9. Jump sideways off a low bench? Try backward.
10. Jump forward off a chair or box and catch a sponge ball in midair and land safely?
11. Jump in different directions off steps, chairs, side horse, Swedish box, and tree stumps?

Balance Beam and Walking Plank Activities

Walking boards, beams, and planks should be an integral

part of your balance program. The boards should be different widths, heights, and inclines to allow challenges for children who progress faster than others. Activities should be geared to the height of the board as the fear-factor comes into play as the board is raised. Children frequently find it difficult to balance themselves on a small walking surface at a height. It is advantageous for the instructor to hold a child under the upper arm when the child is first attempting to walk along the board or is performing a difficult task. Only one child should be allowed on a board at a time.

Can you —

1. Walk forward the length of the board keeping your arms out to the side and focus your eyes on the end of the board?
2. Walk sideways sliding the left foot as the lead leg for the length of the board? Repeat using right foot as the lead.
3. Walk slowly across the board placing your hands on the hips, hands on the head, arms folded across the chest, arms held straight out in front?
4. Walk across the walking board not touching the swinging ball? (A suspendable rubber, plastic, or sponge ball is hung from the ceiling and swung like a pendulum by the instructor perpendicular to the board.)
5. Walk forward to the center of the board and perform a stork stand, a swan stand, or a T-scale?
6. Walk along the board not stepping on bean bags placed one yard apart on the board?
7. Step over a cross bar, which is placed on two traffic cones, across the center of the walking board without touching it?
8. Step over or around traffic cones, which are placed on the board, without touching them or falling off the board?
9. Stoop to pick up bean bags, which are placed one yard apart on the board, while walking the length of the board?
10. Walk forward across the board to the middle, turn around, and continue walking to the end?
11. Balance a bean bag on your head and walk slowly across the board?

12. Walk backwards across the board crossing the feet in a normal backward walking pattern? Keep your head up.
13. Walk forward to the center of the walking board, turn halfway around, and walk backward to the end of the board?
14. Walk forward across the board carrying a bamboo pole like a tight-rope walker?
15. Walk forward across the board carrying plastic painters'

Figure 14. Walking the Beam with an Added Weight.

buckets in each hand. Try filling one bucket with bean bags and attempt walking across the board (fig. 14).

16. Walk across the board and duck under a crossbar, which is placed across the center of the board at shoulder height, without touching it? Try lowering the crossbar to waist height.

17. Walk along the board and go through a hoop, which is held by the instructor in the center of the board, without touching it?

18. Walk forward, backward, and sideways up and down a board that is placed at an incline?

19. Balance on the walking board and play catch, using an 8-inch sponge ball, with the instructor?

20. Balance on the walking board while you bounce and catch an 8-inch playground ball?

21. Balance on one end of the walking board while a partner balances on the other end and play catch with a sponge ball?

22. Bounce an 8-inch playground ball in hoops, which are placed along side of the board, and catch it?

23. Hop the length of the walking board on the right foot? Try the left.

24. Stand facing a partner at opposite ends of the board and walk forward passing your partner without you or your partner falling off the board?

25. Design and practice walking different ways along the walking board through obstacles such as crossbars, cones, bean bags, and hoops?

26. Balance on a plank which is placed on top of inner tubes to form a "Jell-O® board" (fig. 15)?

Figure 15. Jello-O Board.

Horizontal Ladder Activities

The ladder provides the motor development instructor with an easy to use, easy to acquire, and innovative piece of equipment. The tasks involving the ladder are easily adaptable to varying physical abilities. The ladder offers challenging ways to gain better dynamic balance. Children should be reminded, when performing ladder activities, to move at a pace so that their bodies are under control. The instructor should spot children with balance difficulties by holding them under the upper arm.

Can you —

1. Walk forward in the ladder spaces without touching any part of the ladder?
2. Walk forward on the rungs of the ladder (fig. 16)?

Figure 16. Walking on the Rungs of the Ladder.

3. Walk forward straddling the ladder with one foot on

either side of it?

4. Walk forward on one side of the ladder only?
5. Walk forward with one foot on the rungs and the other on the side?
6. Walk sideways on the ladder using either a side or the rungs?
7. Walk backward on the rungs of the ladder?
8. Walk backward straddling the ladder with one foot on either side?
9. Straddle the ladder with one foot on each side, walk slowly forward, and bounce and catch an 8-inch rubber playground ball between the rungs?
10. Walk on the rungs of the ladder while tossing a playground ball up into the air and catching it?
11. Stand facing a partner at opposite ends of the ladder and walk forward on the rungs or the side rails and pass the partner without you or your partner falling off?
12. Place the ladder at a higher level or at an incline and perform all walking activities previously listed?

Scooter Board Activities

Scooter boards can be made or purchased commercially and are useful balance tools (fig. 17). The child can ride the scooter boards in a variety of ways to increase the ability to maintain

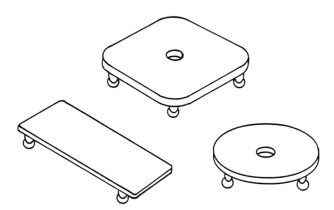

Figure 17. Scooter Boards.

equilibrium while in motion. Children should not be allowed to stand on the scooter boards and should be careful where they place their fingers so they do not pinch them in the rotating coasters or wheels.

Can you —

1. Sit on the scooter board moving forward using just your hands, just your feet, or both hands and feet?
2. Sit on the scooter board moving backward using just your hands, just your feet, or both your hands and feet?
3. Lie in prone position on the scooter moving forward using just your hands, just your feet, or both your hands and feet?
4. Lie in a supine position on the scooter moving in any way, being careful not to bump into anything or anyone?
5. Sit on the scooter and have a partner push you around the floor? (If the pusher is a child, he may go too close to walls. It is important to monitor this type of activity.)
6. Lie on the scooter and have a partner hold on to your ankles and pull you around the floor.
7. Ride the scooter while sitting or lying on it as the instructor pulls you around the floor by use of a rope or bamboo pole?
8. Ride the scooter being pulled by a rope or pole, in and out of traffic cones set up as an obstacle course, around the floor?
9. Ride the scooter in a circle as the instructor pulls you in a circular pattern?
10. Lie on the scooter and use your feet to push off a wall and see how far you can go?
11. Run with hands on the scooter and then jump on to the scooter in prone position or kneeling to go for a ride?
12. Use two plumbers helpers (plungers) to move yourself around the floor on the scooter in a sitting or kneeling position?

Balance Board Activities

Balance boards serve as effective equipment in demonstrating to the user that the balance point must remain in the base to maintain balance. The boards come in different sizes and shapes ranging from the teeter board, in which two sides must be balanced in seesaw fashion, to a traditional balance board, in which four sides are balanced (fig. 18). Boards with smaller or rounded bases demand a greater skill than those with large or flat bases. Children need little supervision when using the boards, thus, the boards lend themselves to "station usage."

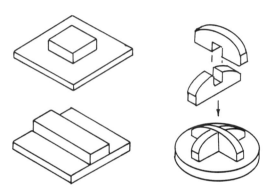

Figure 18. Balance Boards.

Can you —

1. Stand on the balance board, keeping it level, so that none of the sides touch the ground?
2. Balance on the board placing your hands on your hips, hands on the head, arms folded across the chest, arms held straight over head, or with arms held straight out in front?
3. Balance on the board touching the front of the board to the floor, the back of the board to the floor, the back of the board to the floor, or each side of the board to the floor?
4. Take small steps and turn around without falling off the board?
5. Jump off the board forward, backward, or sideways?
6. Balance on the board with a bean bag on your head?
7. Stoop, while you are balancing, to pick up bean bags placed around the board?
8. Balance on the board using just the right foot? Try the left foot.

9. Bounce an 8-inch playground ball while balancing on the board?

10. Play catch with a partner while you both balance on boards?

11. Stand on the board and pop soap bubbles as the instructor blows them towards you?

12. Stand on the board and hit a balloon into the air without the board or the balloon touching the ground?

Jumping Ball Activities

The jumping ball is a large inflated rubber or plastic ball with an attached handle that is commercially sold under a

Figure 19. Bouncing on the Jumping Ball.

variety of names and in different sizes (fig. 19). It is a piece of equipment that the children enjoy immensely, while at the same time they are developing necessary balance skills. Activities such as simple tag games and relay races are readily adaptable to jumping balls. Jumping ball activities can include bouncing on lines and markers, bouncing while performing eye-hand skills such as striking a ball or catching, and bouncing through, over, and around obstacles.

Barrel Activities

Barrels can be easily obtained in different sizes and materials. Cardboard, wooden, or metal barrels can be used by children to roll on while maintaining equilibrium. The child can sit astride the barrel and, by shifting the weight of the body, try to roll the barrel. Children may also perform eye-hand activities while balancing on a barrel.

Large Ball Activities

Large, commercially sold plastic or rubber inflatable balls can be ideally used for activities pertaining to balance. Children can sit on the ball trying not to touch the floor with their hands or feet. They may attempt to perform a Russian or Cossack dance while seated on the ball. By squeezing the ball with the legs, the child can bounce in jumping ball fashion. Rolling on top of the ball while lying on it in a prone position can stimulate a vestibular response (fig. 20).

Figure 20. Balancing on the Large Ball.

One-legged Stool Activity

A one-legged stool can be constructed and used often. Children can sit on the one-legged stool and keep their balance while waiting to participate in an activity, while the instructor is giving directions, or at a station (fig. 21). The stools can be used when performing eye-hand or eye-foot activities.

Figure 21. Balancing on the One-legged Stool.

Activities Involving Stilts

Blocks of wood or strong metal cans with ropes attached provide an appropriate lead-up for stilt walking (fig. 22). These low stilts can be used at a station for children to practice walking in different directions, over and under obstacles, and up and down stairs. Low and high stilt walking provides a rewarding experience for those who learn how to perform the skill. All stilt walking activities should be monitored carefully by the instructor.

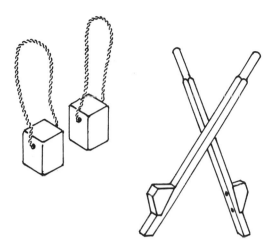

Figure 22. Stilts.

Scooter Activities

The scooter is a superb lead-up to bicycle riding (fig. 23). Children can ride the scooter in clockwise and counterclockwise directions or in and out of traffic cones and other obstacles. The scooter can be utilized in developing balance on one foot by having the child lift the push leg and hold it to the side or straight in back while riding the scooter. He should alternate push feet as well as direction when riding.

Figure 23. The Scooter.

Bicycle Activities

Since bicycling is such an enjoyable lifetime activity and so valuable a means of transportation for children, it is important that each child develop the capability to ride a bike (fig. 24). Although it is a difficult skill for some children, with proper supervision and energetic instruction, the vast majority of students will learn at a young age.

Figure 24. Learning to Ride.

One widely used technique for developing the ability to ride a bike is the use of training wheels. Training wheels are effective, but the instructor must be careful not to let the child become dependent on them, particularly when steering around a corner as balance skills improve. It is necessary that the child trust the instructor so that fear does not hamper the development of riding skill. When teaching the child, the instructor should place one hand on the back of the bicycle seat and the other hand on the handlebar. The teacher should jog with the child, making sure that the child's pedaling action provides the force to move the bike. As the child rides, the instructor should take his hand off the handlebar to let the child practice steering, but continue to hold on to the seat to provide momentum. If this skill can be accomplished, the instructor should release the hand on the bike seat while holding on to the handlebar with one hand. Children must be reminded to keep their feet on the pedals and keep pushing. If the child can perform these two skills and the instructor feels the child is ready, the instructor can let the child go in a straight line while keeping the hands close to the seat and handlebars. Although it is important for the child to ride the bike alone, it helps if the instructor can run beside the child for safety reasons when the child is first learning.

Balance Equipment Alternatives

With imagination, an instructor can find many useful and fun activities for the development of balance. Roller skates, ice skates, pogo sticks, and skateboards are all balance equipment that can be utilized with careful supervision and instruction.

Chapter 5

EYE-HAND COORDINATION

Figure 25. Suspendable Ball Striking Bowling Pins.

EYE-HAND coordination combines the use of the hands and eyes working together to accomplish a task. Training in this area includes the ability to strike, roll, throw, catch, and push objects in the appropriate manner. Eye-tracking is very important in all of these areas. Children need to learn how to judge moving objects, such as balls, beanbags, and other apparatus, so that they can comfortably handle themselves when confronted with eye-hand activities in games and lifetime situations.

EYE-TRACKING ACTIVITIES

Suspendable Ball

A ball can be suspended in midair by attaching a string to a ball (rubber, sponge, plastic with holes) and hanging it from a ceiling or tree branch.

1. The child stands in front of the ball that is suspended in the air at waist level. The ball is swung back and forth, and he attempts to touch or catch the ball. The height of the ball can be changed to increase the difficulty of the task.
2. The child tries to touch or catch the ball as it swings in a circular motion. Vary the height of the ball.
3. The child tries to touch or catch the ball that is swung in different directions while he lies down on his back in a supine position below the ball.

Flashlight

1. Move a flashlight beam randomly on a wall and have the child point to the light as it moves.
2. Using a flashlight beam, trace letters, numbers, and shapes on the wall for the child to follow.
3. The child uses a flashlight to follow a swinging suspended ball.

Marble Machine

This wooden marble rolling piece of equipment can be

bought or made rather inexpensively (fig. 26). A marble is dropped in a slot and rolls down wooden slats until it reaches the bottom tray.

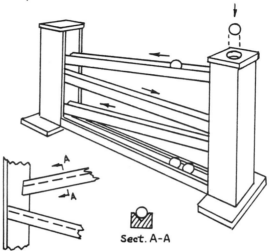

Figure 26. Marble Machine.

Figure 27. Stopping the Marble.

1. The marble is placed in the starting hole and the child is asked to follow the marble with his eyes until it reaches the bottom tray.
2. As the marble rolls down the slats, the child is asked to use his finger to stop the marble on a specific slat (fig. 27).
3. As several marbles roll down the slats, the child is asked to stop a specific color marble before it reaches the bottom tray.

Rolling

Log Roll

Using two or more tumbling mats, the child lies down across a mat with the hands extended over the head and the legs together. He must roll from front to back continuously down the length of the mats.

Barrel Rolls

1. The child gets inside a barrel and performs a series of log rolls to move the barrel across the play area.
2. Using two hands, the child rolls a barrel in a straight line, very fast, slowly, under control while changing directions, and in a circle.

Dowel Rolls

1. The child rolls dowels in a crooked line, a straight line, forward, sideways, and using one and two hands.
2. The child tries to knock down a target (juice container, bowling pin) by rolling a dowel at it.

Playground Balls

Using 8- to 10-inch playground balls and other different size balls,
Can you —

1. Use two hands to roll a ball while you run behind it?

2. Roll a ball slowly?
3. Roll a ball quickly and try to run past it?
4. Roll a ball in a straight line?
5. Roll a ball using only one hand?
6. Roll a ball at a target using only one hand?
7. Roll a ball at a specified number that is among several numbers marked on the floor?
8. Roll a ball at a specified letter that is among several letters marked on the floor?
9. Roll a ball at a specified color that is among several pieces of colored paper spread out on the floor?
10. Roll a ball to a partner?
11. Use a 30-inch ball to roll back and forth to a partner?

Bowling

Using a commercially purchased or homemade bowling set, children can try to knock pins down by rolling a ball at them. To make sure that the child will be successful in the activity, the line from which the ball is released is close to the pins. If it is too easy to knock the pins down, the line should be moved back. The formation of the pins can be marked on the floor for easy reference. Stress keeping the eyes on the pins, rolling the ball in a straight line, stepping forward with the opposite leg, following through with the arm, and bending at the knees.

Striking

Soap Bubbles

The child pops bubbles with the fingers, left hand, right hand, arms, and elbows (fig. 28). The child pops bubbles by clapping the hands together, grasping the bubbles with the hand, and by hitting them with a plastic bat or a cardboard tube.

Figure 28. Popping the Soap Bubbles.

Suspended Balloons

Attach a thin wire or rope along the width of the gymnasium, cafeteria, or room at a height of approximately seven feet. Tie strings to large round balloons and hang them from the wire.

1. The child hits the balloon upward by striking it with the right hand and then the left hand.
2. The child hits the balloon forward by striking it on the side with the left and right hand.
3. The child punches the balloons with alternating hands.
4. The child uses a paddle or paper plate to hit the balloon. Try using a badminton racquet or Ping-Pong® paddle (fig. 29).

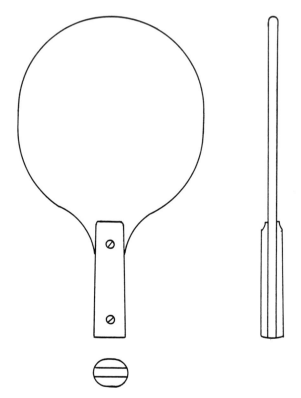

Figure 29. Ping-Pong Paddle.

5. The child uses cardboard dowels, rolled newspaper, or plastic bat to hit the balloon with a baseball swing.

Balloons

1. The child hits a balloon with his right hand, left hand, and alternating hands.
2. The child keeps the balloon in the air as long as possible without catching it, using just the hands to hit the balloon.
3. Using a paddle, the child hits the balloon into the air as many times as possible.
4. Using a plastic baseball bat, the child hits the balloon into the air.
5. Using a paddle to keep the balloon aloft, the child hits the balloon into boxes, milk crates, or through hoops.
6. Using a table or bench as a net, the child plays balloon tennis with a partner. Each child must hit the balloon across the net to the other side.

Suspendable Balls

1. Using a paddle with either the left hand or the right hand, the child hits the ball (fig. 30A).
2. The child hits the ball using a forehand stroke with a paddle (fig. 30B).
3. The child attempts to hit the ball as many times as possible consecutively.
4. With a partner, the child takes turns hitting the ball with a paddle.
5. Using a large plastic bat, the child swings baseball style at the suspended ball, hitting it in the same direction every time (fig. 30C).

Figure 30. Striking the Suspendable Ball with (A) the Hand, (B) a Paddle, or (C) a Plastic Bat.

Tetherball

The child can hit or punch the tetherball so that it spins around the pole. A paddle or racquet can be used and partners can practice hitting the ball back and forth or compete in a tetherball game.

Batting Tee

1. Using a large beach ball placed on a batting tee, the child strikes the ball by punching it with a clenched fist. A modified baseball game can be played.
2. The child strikes an 8-inch plastic ball with a clenched fist or open hand.
3. The child hits a ball off a batting tee using a paddle. Start with a large lightweight plastic ball and progress to a smaller ball (fig. 31).

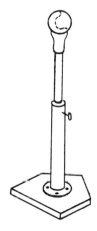

Figure 31. Batting Tee.

4. Using a large plastic bat, the child hits a ball off the batting tee. Proper baseball swing technique including hand position, foot placement, weight transfer, and level of swing should be emphasized.
5. Using a thin plastic bat, the child hits a plastic ball off the tee. If the area of play is large enough, a wooden bat and

fleece-filled softball may be tried.

Throwing and Catching

Effective throwing involves keeping the eyes on the target, using proper hand and foot positions, and appropriate follow through. A proficient catcher keeps his eyes on the object being thrown at all times, keeps his hands outstretched to meet the ball, and cushions the ball by bringing it back towards the body when the catch is made.

Two Hand Side Throw

The ball is held in front of the body with the fingers spread around the ball. Bending the elbows, the arms are swung to the side as far back as possible. Swing the ball forward, shifting the body weight to the forward foot, releasing the ball from both hands.

Two Hand Underhand Throw

The ball is held in front of the body with feet in a stride position and weight evenly distributed on both feet. The ball is brought between the legs with elbows slightly bent and then pushed forward and upward, releasing the ball from both hands.

Two Hand Overhand Throw

The child holds the ball in both hands over the head, with the legs apart and the weight evenly distributed on both feet. With one foot slightly in front of the other, the weight is shifted on the back leg with the ball behind the head. The child swings both arms forward in front of the head, shifting the weight to the front leg and releasing the ball.

One Hand Overhand Throw

With one leg slightly in front of the other (opposite from

throwing arm) and the weight evenly distributed on both feet, the child shifts the weight to the back foot. The ball is brought upward above the shoulder and behind the ear. The child swings the hand forward, shifting the weight to the front foot, and releases the ball as the arm is outstretched.

Two Hand Underhand Catch

The child spreads his feet apart slightly, bends the elbows, and spreads his fingers apart. He steps to meet the ball with the arms extended forward and the hands apart about the width of the ball. The ball should be caught with the finger and thumb tips. As the ball is caught, the elbows are bent and the body weight shifts to the back foot bringing the ball close to the body.

Two Hand Overhand Catch

The child stands with the feet slightly apart and the elbows bent. The fingers are spread open with the palms of the hands facing away from the child. The child extends the arms forward to meet the ball, catching it with the fingertips. He should bend the elbows to bring the ball close to the body.

Bean Bags

Can you —

1. Toss a bean bag in the air just above your head with two hands and catch it?
2. Toss a bean bag in the air with the left hand? Try your right hand.
3. Toss a bean bag from one hand to the other?
4. Throw a bean bag at a target using one hand or two hands either overhand or underhand? Targets can be hoops, boxes, milk cartons, rug samples, alphabet letters, tires, bowling pins, or taped targets on the wall or floor.
5. Toss a bean bag to a partner throwing it with your right hand and catching it with your left? Try throwing with the left and catching with the right.

6. Toss a bean bag back and forth with a partner playing follow the leader in throwing and catching methods?
7. Toss a bean bag to a partner as he tosses one to you?
8. Toss a bean bag to a partner and clap your hands after you throw and before you catch your partner's bean bag?

Wands

Can you —

1. Hold the wand in both hands at waist level, palms facing up, and toss the wand into the air and catch it?
2. Toss and catch the wand over the head continuously for one minute without letting the wand drop to the ground?
3. Toss the wand with your left hand and catch it? Now try your right hand.
4. Toss and catch the wand with a partner?
5. Form a circle with other children and toss a wand around the circle without dropping it?

Playground Balls

Can you —

1. Throw a ball into the air, let it bounce and catch it?

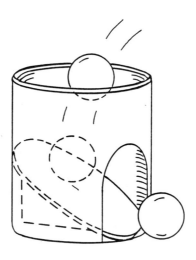

Figure 32. Ball-Return Container.

2. Throw a ball to a partner five or more feet away using underhand, side arm, or overhand throwing techniques?
3. Throw a ball underhand and overhand into a large container? Now try throwing into a smaller container. Try cutting a large hole at the bottom of the container and inserting a false bottom at an angle. The balls will then return to you (fig. 32).
5. Throw a ball at a wall, clap your hands, let the ball bounce, and catch it?

Pushing and Dribbling

A pushing motion is a difficult concept to learn, since children tend to strike at an object rather than guide it. The skill of dribbling a ball is a pushing activity that can be best learned by starting with a large plastic ball. When dribbling a ball, the child's body should lean forward slightly, knees bent, feet spread shoulders width apart, and the weight distributed evenly on both feet. As the child pushes the ball down with the fingers, the instructor can guide the child's hand to get the feeling of pushing the ball, not slapping it. As the child learns to push down to dribble, a smaller ball can be used.

Shuffleboard

Children can practice pushing the shuffleboard stick forward and learn to push the shuffleboard disc rather than hit it (fig. 33). Children can shoot the disc aiming at numbers, letters, or colors. Recreational shuffleboard can be modified, and children can use two hands, the left hand, and right hand.

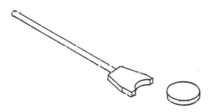

Figure 33. Shuffleboard Stick and Disc.

Hockey

Plastic hockey sticks and pucks can be bought commercially. Drills, relay races, and games can be set up to teach the child to push the hockey puck while keeping it under control. The push shot and wrist shot technique will aid children in gaining the feel of pushing rather than striking at objects.

Playground Balls

Can you —

1. Bounce and catch a playground ball as you move around the play area?
2. Dribble a playground ball six times consecutively?
3. Dribble a playground ball while moving forward, backward, or sideways?
4. Dribble a ball in and out of obstacles such as cones, hoops, or rug samples?
5. Dribble a ball while lying down, kneeling, or standing on your toes?
6. Dribble a ball with just your right hand, two hands, left hand, and switching hands?
7. Dribble while moving very quickly around the play area?

EYE-HAND COORDINATION GAMES

Circle Bean Bag

Children are divided into equal teams that form two circles. A bean bag is given to the captain of each team. The instructor selects the number of trips the bean bags are to take around the circle. On the signal, the captain passes the bean bag to the player on his right, who in turn passes it to the next player, and so on around the circle. When the bean bag returns to the captain he calls out loudly, "one" signifying that one trip has been made. The game continues until one team has completed the designated number of trips. The game can be played by asking the children to throw the bean bag with the left hand, right hand, overhand, underhand, etc.

Circle Ball

Children form a circle leaving a space between each child. A ball is passed to each player in turn around the circle. Once the ball is started, a second ball can be introduced and passed around in the same or different direction.

Bridge Roll

Two traffic cones are set up one foot apart with a dowel or stick placed across the top of the cones, forming a bridge between the two. Two children sit facing one another with the bridge in between them. Each child sits approximately four feet from the cone bridge. The children see how many times they can roll a ball between the cones without knocking the dowel off the cones. The game can be changed by having children move farther away from the cones or by moving the cones closer together.

Human Wicket

Children form a circle with each player's legs in a stride position forming a wicket. One child is chosen to stand in the center of the circle with the ball. He attempts to roll the ball between the legs of any player in the circle or between any two players. The players in the circle may use their hands to stop the ball, however, they cannot move their feet. If the circle player fails to stop the ball from rolling out of the circle, he or she becomes the roller in the middle.

Target Ball

Teams line up at opposite ends of the play area with each player on a team having a ball. On the starting signal, children throw balls at the center ball trying to push the ball over the opposing team's line. When a team does push the ball over the other team's line they are awarded one point. If the ball goes over the side lines, a kicker may be placed at either side line to kick the ball in bounds. The team with the greatest number of points wins. Children can be asked to roll balls, throw them underhand, or overhand. Different size balls can be used (fig. 34).

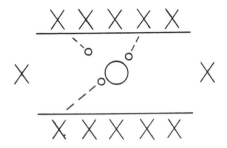

Figure 34. Target Ball.

Roll Ball

Four bases are set up in play area with a bowling pin, club, or box set up at home plate. Children are divided into teams and each player's turn consists of three tries to knock the object down at home plate to get on base. If the child misses it, an "out" is given to the team. Teams switch places designating an inning, when everybody on the rolling team gets one turn.

Bean Bag Throw

Children line up behind a throwing line. On the signal from the instructor, children throw the bean bags as far as possible. After all bean bags have been thrown, each child retrieves his own. Different methods of throwing (overhand, underhand) can be used as well as targets added.

Bean Bag Line Catch

One child stands 10 feet in front of a line of children. He throws a bean bag underhand at waist level to each child in the line. Each child in the line catches the bean bag and returns it. Repeat until all children have had a turn. The leader then goes to the end of the line, and the next player in line takes his place as leader. Balls, sponge cubes, and different methods of throwing and catching may be used.

Ball Toss

Children stand in a large circle with one child in the middle with a playground ball. The child in the middle tosses the ball up in the air calling out another child's name. The child whose name is called runs into the middle and tries to catch the ball. He calls a name and tosses the ball in the air.

Balloon Volleyball

The game is played like volleyball except the net is lowered, and a balloon is used. The balloon is hit by the server and there is no limit to the amount of times the balloon is hit on each side (fig. 35). As the players improve, the number of hits on each side can be limited.

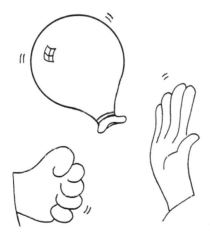

Figure 35. Balloon Volleyball.

Modified Baseball

The instructor pitches a large plastic ball, using an under-hand motion, to the child who attempts to strike the ball with an oversized plastic bat. As the child becomes proficient at this activity, a smaller ball and thinner bat can be utilized.

Modified Handball

Partners using an 8-inch playground ball hit the ball back and forth across a line with an open hand (fig. 36). When beginning, each player may hit the ball after it bounces twice on their side. After competency is developed, one bounce is allowed on a side.

Figure 36. Modified Handball.

Balloon Badminton

Playing a game similar to badminton, children see how many times a balloon can be hit over a lowered net using badminton racquets.

Balloon Soccer

Children are divided into two teams and one child from each team is a goalie who stands between two cones, which represent the goal. The instructor throws a balloon up in the center of the playing field and players begin to strike the balloon. They are not allowed to run with the balloon or hit it more than once in succession. When the balloon goes past the cones and the goalie, a point is scored.

Bean Bag Volleyball

A volleyball net is set up according to the height of the children, and a sponge ball, plastic ball, playgound ball, or a bean bag is used in playing the game. The players throw the ball over the net (underhand, overhand), and the other team catches the ball and throws it back.

Catch a Bat

Children form a circle with one child in the middle. The child in the middle calls out the name of one of the members of the circle and then lets go of a bat that he is balancing on the floor. The child whose name was called should rush into the middle and attempt to catch the bat, pole, or wand before it falls. If the bat is caught, the child stays in the center and calls another name (fig. 37).

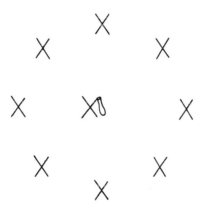

Figure 37. Catch a Bat.

Horseshoes

Rubber horseshoes can be commercially bought. Set the horseshoes up ten feet apart and have the child try to get the horseshoe as close to the target as possible, trying to make a ringer. Child should keep his eyes on the target, throw with one hand underhand, and take a step forward. The distance can be increased as accuracy increases.

Dodge Ball

Children are divided into two teams, one team forming a circle as the other team stands inside the circle. Using a sponge or plastic ball, the children forming a circle throw the ball at those inside. If an insider is struck by the ball, he takes his place as a thrower on the edge of the circle. When everyone has been hit, the original throwers switch places with the dodgers.

Deck Tennis

Set up a volleyball net the appropriate height for the age and ability of the children playing the game. A deck tennis ring is thrown over the net and children on the other side try to catch it. If the catch is successful, the child throws it back over the net. When a ring hits the ground or goes outside, it is a miss. Points are scored by serving team only as in regulation volleyball. Children must be reminded to stay in their own area. Hoops and rug samples can be set up so that children must have at least one foot in a hoop or on a rug to prevent players leaving their positions.

Sticky Ball

A 4- to 6-inch foam ball can be covered with double faced tape or the commercially designed "sticky" cloth. One child can be the thrower, and his partner can wear a cloth mitt to catch the ball (fig. 38).

Figure 38. Catching the "Sticky" Ball.

Scoop Throwing

Scoops can be made out of plastic gallon milk jugs or bought commercially. Children can experiment with throwing and catching a variety of balls (Ping-Pong®, whiffle, sponge) with a partner.

Flying Discs

Commercially purchased flying discs can be enjoyed by partners or in groups. They can be thrown at targets such as boxes or milk cartons or through hoops. Games such as flying disc golf or flying disc baseball can also be played.

Chapter 6

EYE-FOOT COORDINATION

Figure 39. Foot Placement.

EYE-FOOT coordination combines the use of the feet and eyes working together to accomplish an appointed task. Children need to become aware of their feet and their fundamental movement characteristics. The activities involved in improving balance and locomotor skill can also be used to improve eye-foot coordination.

Foot Placement

Footprints

Footprints can be purchased commercially or made out of cardboard, plastic, or rubber. Child can practice walking or performing various locomotor skills on evenly spaced footprints. The prints can be numbered or color coded and the child must walk in specific patterns.

Obstacle Course

Set up an obstacle course using chairs, tires, hoops, footprints, boxes, and ropes, and have child move through the course maintaining balance.

Tires

Moving in a zig-zag pattern, the child weaves around and in between tires by running, skipping, galloping, hopping, jumping, and sliding.

Hopscotch

The traditional game of hopscotch will aid the child in foot placement and balance.

Kicking

Balloons

The child kicks a balloon into the air and tries to keep it aloft using only the feet.

Bean Bag

The child pushes the bean bag across the floor with his feet using just the right foot or the left foot. Draw or mark circles with numbers, letters, and colors on the floor. Have the child stand on a starting line and kick the bean bag towards the targets.

Ladder

The child, using just his feet, moves the ball from one space between the rungs of a ladder to the next.

Playground Balls

Can you —

1. Keep your eyes on the ball, step into the ball, and kick it with your toe?
2. Kick a stationary ball at a target on a wall?
3. Kick a ball that is rolled by the instructor directly at you?
4. Kick a ball using the instep of the foot?
5. Kick a ball with the outside of the foot?
6. Kick a ball with the back of the foot?
7. Kick a ball to a partner with the toe, instep, ouside, and back of the foot?
8. Kick a ball that is bouncing directly in front of you?

Dribbling

Playground Balls

Can you —

1. Dribble a ball using the instep of the foot, keeping the ball close to the foot?
2. Dribble a ball alternating feet with each kick of the ball?
3. Dribble a ball using the toe of each foot?
4. Dribble a ball using the outside of each foot?
5. Dribble a ball around cones, hoops, rugs, and other obstacles?

6. Dribble a ball and on a given signal stop dribbling it by trapping it?

EYE-FOOT COORDINATION GAMES

Kick the Wall

The group is divided into two teams with a line dividing the playing area. Each team must stay on their half of the area and try to score points by kicking the ball towards their opponent's wall. Each time the ball strikes the opposite wall a point is scored. The teams can defend their wall only by trapping the ball with their feet or body.

Kick-off

Children scatter behind a line and are fielders. One child is chosen to be a kicker and the instructor is the catcher. The kicker kicks the ball into the field, runs to a base and back to home again. The fielders attempt to catch the ball and throw it to the instructor/catcher before the kicker returns to home base. If the kicker tags the base before the instructor catches the ball, he is awarded another kick. The fielder who catches the ball first becomes the next kicker, if the player is out. If the kicker is out or had two chances to kick, he becomes a fielder (fig. 40).

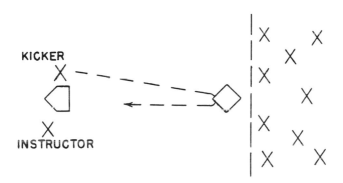

Figure 40. Kick-off.

Team Effort

Children form groups of three and hold hands. A ball is placed in front of each team of three and the object of the game is for the team to dribble the ball to a designated area as quickly as possible without letting go of hands. Each team can race against other teams or race against the clock.

Modified Soccer

This game can be played either indoors or outdoors. Depending on the age of the group playing, you may be able to incorporate many regulation soccer rules.

The group should be divided into two teams and a goal marked at each end to be defended. The most important rule will be that only the feet can be used to move the ball towards the goal. If the ball passes through the marked goal, a point is scored. A foam soccer ball can be purchased for indoor use.

Kick and Run

Children are divided into two teams. One team is at home plate, while the other team acts as the fielders. The ball is rolled to the first person at home plate and he kicks it and tries to run the bases before he is hit by the ball or before one of the fielders reaches a base before he does. Each person on the team gets a chance to kick and then the teams switch places.

Kick Golf

Construction paper circles, bases, plastic letters, or traffic cones can be placed around the play area, each with a number form one to nine on it. Children start at a designated spot and, by kicking a sponge ball or cube, count how many kicks it takes to hit item number one. The child then kicks the ball at item number two and so on until he reaches nine. The child with the least amount of kicks wins.

Chapter 7

FINE-MOTOR COORDINATION

Figure 41. Lacing, Buckling, Zipping, and Snapping.

Eye-HAND coordination using the small muscles is equally as important as gross-motor skills. Motor learning usually sequences from gross skills to fine, and this should be kept in mind when teaching fine-motor skills. If a child's basic gross-motor skills haven't developed, chances are his fine-motor skills will also be poor.

Poor fine-motor ability can be the result of one of three factors or a combination of any. The child may not have the small muscle strength to perform the tasks, he may have poor finger-hand dexterity, or his eyes may not be able to follow the activity.

The following activities should help in developing fine-motor ability in children.

Activities Dealing with the Fine Muscles

Page Fanning

Give the child a hard cover book and ask him to turn the pages one by one.

Keyboard Walking

If a piano is available, have the child walk his fingers up and down the keyboard.

Toothpick Play

Using large wooden toothpicks, have the child make different shapes and forms on a flat surface. Pile the toothpicks up, and have the child pick each one up without moving the rest of the toothpicks in the pile.

Sewing Cards

You can make cards using heavy cardboard or purchase them commercially. The child should choose cards with simple patterns at first and then progress to more complex patterns.

Coin Counting

Give the child a pile of coins and have him sort and stack them.

Peg Board

Pegs can be placed in the board holes randomly, according to color, or following patterns (fig. 42).

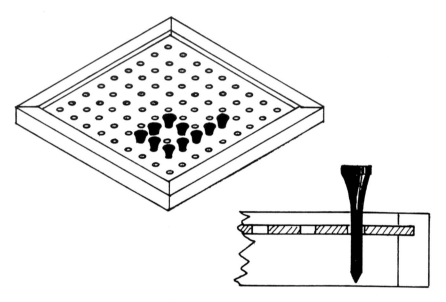

Figure 42. Peg Board.

Channel Drawing

Channels are made by drawing parallel lines on pages, and the child is asked to draw with accuracy between them (fig. 43). After straight lines are followed with some degree of accuracy, the child can be presented with more difficult curved lines. The distance between the parallel lines can gradually be decreased to one quarter of an inch.

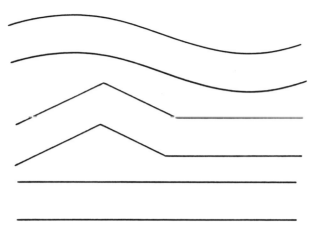

Figure 43. Channel Drawing.

Workbench

A child's workbench can be used for hammering and screwing with child-size tools.

Squeezing to Music

Using a small rubber ball or a hand-grip strengthener, the child can squeeze in time to music and strengthen the small muscles.

Paper Crumpling

Place a piece of paper on a flat surface and have the child gather and crumple the paper into a ball by using just one hand. After sufficient skill has been developed, the child can be handed the paper and, without the aid of the flat surface, he can crumple it into a ball (fig. 44).

Figure 44. Paper Crumbling.

Clay Molding

The child can mold a piece of clay into a ball. He can then make a snake by rolling the piece of clay between his hands. Other shapes and forms can later be designed.

Cardboard Bending

Using small cardboard scraps, the child can bend them into as many angles as possible.

Paper Punch

Using a paper punch, the child punches holes in a piece of paper. He may do this at random or follow a set design.

Finger Painting

Using finger paints, the child can paint and scribble using his fingers.

Clothespin Activities

Using a spring clothespin, the child can open and close it with the thumb and each of the fingers. He can squeeze it open and clip it on to an edge of a box and then squeeze it open again to remove it.

Scissor Cutting

Supply the child with appropriate size scissors, and show him how to hold and cut with them. Give him several sheets of paper to cut at random.

Bead Stringing

Give the child some string and beads with large holes. He can string the beads at random or according to color or shape.

Dot Connection

Dots can be placed on a page in various patterns. The child can connect the dots with lines that may be vertical, horizontal, or in a curve, depending upon where the dots are placed.

Mazes

Books of mazes can be bought commercially, or you can design your own ranging from simple to more complex (fig. 45).

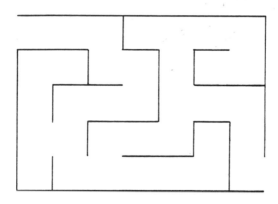

Figure 45. Mazes.

Busy Box

Boxes can be made that require zipping, lacing, buttoning, tying, snapping, and buckling.

Yarn Cards

Cards can be designed that have yarn glued to the surface in different shapes, letters, and numbers. The child is blindfolded and asked to distinguish what shape the yarn is in.

Table Soccer

The game can be made or purchased commercially (fig. 46). Children can play the game trying to score the ping pong ball into the opponent's goal. Eye-tracking as well as fine-motor dexterity can be developed while playing the game.

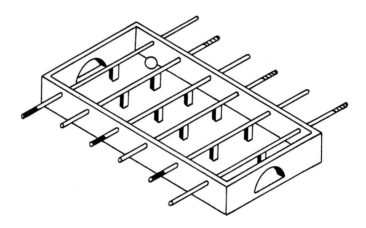

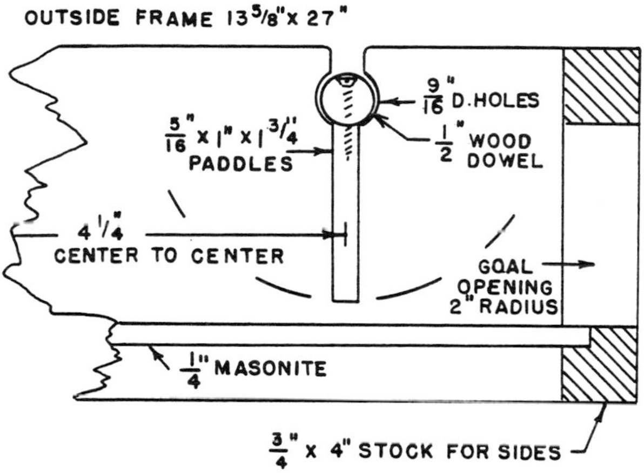

OUTSIDE FRAME 13⅝"x 27"

$\frac{9}{16}$" D.HOLES

$\frac{1}{2}$" WOOD DOWEL

$\frac{5}{16}$" x 1" x 1¾" PADDLES

4¼" CENTER TO CENTER

GOAL OPENING 2" RADIUS

$\frac{1}{4}$" MASONITE

$\frac{3}{4}$" x 4" STOCK FOR SIDES

Figure 46. Table Soccer.

Chapter 8

LOCOMOTOR SKILLS

Figure 47. Leaping Over the Hurdles.

LOCOMOTOR skills deals with an individual's ability to move his body through space. A fine combination of strength, coordination, and balance is needed to move the body from one position to another as efficiently as possible. A gymnast's handspring, a dancer's leap, or a track athlete's running stride require a great deal of locomotor skill to accomplish easily and seemingly with little effort. This skill can be enhanced by a gradual introduction of activities that are designed around the idea of increasing the degree of difficulty in order to improve performance.

Walking Activities

Can you —

1. Walk softly, placing your heels down first, pointing your toes forward?
2. Walk up on your toes keeping your balance?
3. Walk at different speeds (fast, slow)?
4. Walk at different levels (high, medium, low)?
5. Walk demonstrating different moods (happy, sad)?
6. Walk in one direction and on a signal by the instructor, walk in another direction?
7. Walk like a robot, swinging your left arm and left leg forward simultaneously and right arm and right leg next?
8. Walk swinging the arms alternately in opposition to the forward foot?
9. Walk sideways?
10. Walk like a monkey, letting your hands hang low and bending at the knees?
11. Walk like you were going against a strong wind?
12. Walk backward, placing one foot behind the other?

Running Activities

Can you —

1. Run on the balls of your feet, pointing your feet straight ahead, leaning slightly forward?
2. Run at different heights or levels (high, medium, low)?

3. Run and stop on a signal given by the instructor?
4. Run very fast pumping your elbows back and forth?
5. Run and change direction on a signal?
6. Run repeatedly to the count of six, each time going further than the time before?
7. Run low to the ground and increase your level of height until you are running as high as possible?
8. Run while raising your knees very high?
9. Run as if you were being chased, catching a train, or were an airplane or bird?

Jumping Activities

Can you —

1. Bend at the knees, crouching low, jump off one foot landing on two feet?
2. Bend at the knees, crouching low, jump off two feet landing on two feet?
3. Jump high into the air and land softly on two feet?
4. Run and jump over a line?
5. Run and jump into a box mat or crash pad landing on your seat?
6. Jump and turn while in the air?
7. Jump, swinging your arms forward and up?
8. Jump backward?
9. Jump in different directions (forward, sideways, backward)?
10. Jump in the direction that the instructor points (sideways, to the right or left, forward, or backward)?
11. Jump a minimal amount of times to get from one place to another?
12. Jump as if you were a frog, a kangaroo, or a grasshopper?

Leaping Activities

Can you —

1. Run and take off on one foot landing softly on the other?

2. Run gaining maximum height with every running stride you take?
3. Run and leap forward with your right foot? Now try your left.
4. Run quickly taking little steps then leap forward?
5. While holding hands with a partner, run and leap together?
6. Run and leap on a signal given by the instructor?
7. Leap across the ground pretending you are a giant, Big Foot, Paul Bunyon, or a bionic person?
8. Leap over a line landing on two feet and fall forward?
9. Leap over an object (tire, hoop) and land on one foot without losing your balance?
10. Step over a plastic wand or plastic hockey stick placed between two traffic cones? Now leap over it.
11. Leap over a series of small traffic cone hurdles, taking off on one foot and landing on the other foot each time you go over a hurdle?
12. Run and leap over a series of low hurdles?

Hopping Activities

Can you —

1. Hop by pushing off on one foot and land softly on the same foot?
2. Hop ten times on your right foot staying in the same place?
3. Hop as high as you can on each foot?
4. Hop as far as you can on each foot?
5. Hop sideways without losing your balance?
6. Hop spinning around in a circle?
7. Hop backward?
8. Take quick short hops and then take slow big hops?
9. Hop, keeping your arms folded across your chest?
10. Run at a medium speed and take one giant hop, taking off on one foot and landing on the same foot?
11. Hop as if you were a rabbit, playing hopscotch, or on hot charcoals?

Sliding Activities

Can you —

1. Slide sideways, not crossing your feet, keeping the same foot in the lead?
2. Slide to the right and on a given signal change direction?
3. Slide taking short strides? Now try long strides.
4. Stand face to face with a partner and slide holding your partner's hands?
5. Stand back to back with a partner and slide holding your partner's hands?
6. Slide in a circle, square, or triangle?
7. Slide as if you were skating?

Galloping Activities

Can you —

1. Gallop by placing one foot ahead of the other, bringing the back foot up to, but not past, the front foot?
2. Gallop in a circle?
3. Gallop at different speeds (fast, medium, slow)?
4. Gallop holding hands with a partner?
5. Gallop using the right foot as the lead leg? Now try the left foot.
6. Gallop, changing the lead leg when the instructor signals?
7. Gallop around objects placed on the floor (cones, hoops, rugs)?
8. Gallop as if you were a horse?

Skipping Activities

Can you —

1. Hop in place on one foot and then the other, alternating feet after each hop?
2. Hop on one foot, then the other, alternating as you move forward?
3. Skip by taking a series of hops? (It may be necessary for

the instructor to hold the child's hand and go through a series of step-hops with the child.)
4. With both hands holding a large ball, skip and raise your knee up to touch the ball, which is held at waist height? Repeat the action with the opposite knee?
5. Skip quickly?
6. Skip along different shapes in the playground area such as a circle, square, or triangle?
7. Skip lightly?
8. Skip taking a minimal amount of steps when trying to get from one point to another?
9. Skip as if you were a clown or a floppy scarecrow?

Climbing Activities

Can you —

1. Ascend and descend a series of steps using an alternate

Figure 48. Climbing the Cargo Net.

stepping pattern?
2. Climb mats stacked to waist level?
3. Climb up a board that is raised two feet at one end.
4. Climb onto a Swedish box?
5. Climb the side rails of a ladder that is placed at a 30 degree angle?
6. Climb four tires that are stacked in a pile?
7. Climb the steps to an outdoor playground slide?
8. Climb a vertical ladder?
9. Climb a set of stall bars?
10. Climb a jungle gym?
11. Climb a rope ladder using a cross pattern motion?
12. Climb a cargo net (fig. 48).
13. Climb a hanging rope?

Tumbling Activities

Can you —
1. Perform a forward roll? Stand at the edge of the mat, squat down, place your hands in front of you with your fingers pointing forward and palms down on the mat. Push forward with your feet, tucking your chin to your chest, keeping your back rounded, and roll forward and over on your back.
2. Roll forward, cross your legs, and stand up by turning your body one half a turn and uncrossing your legs?
3. Roll forward pushing off with your feet and complete with a standing position?
4. Roll forward holding on to an 8-inch playground ball as you roll?
5. Run a few steps, jump off both feet, tuck your chin to your chest and perform a forward roll on a box mat?
6. Start from a stand and do a forward roll coming to a squat position and do another forward roll until you can perform a series of them?
7. Perform a forward roll starting from a standing position executing a forward lunge, taking the body weight on the

hands, so that a dive roll is completed?

8. Run a few steps and dive into a box mat performing a forward roll dive?
9. Run a few steps and dive through a hoop held by the instructor into a box mat completing the task with a forward roll?
10. Jump off a Swedish box landing on two feet, and perform a forward or dive roll?
11. Perform a partial backward roll on the edge of a mat, knees bent, and chin tucked to the chest? Roll backward onto rounded back and shoulders. Placing the hands on the mat, the fingers should be pointing forward with the thumbs close to the body. Rock on the spine, back and forth, placing the hands in the proper position on the mat.

Individual Stunts

Bear Walk

Walk on all fours, facing the floor, keeping the legs and arms straight.

Duck Waddle

Walk in a squat position, keeping knees apart, back straight, and head high. Place the hands on top of shoulders, bending at the elbows for wings (fig. 49).

Figure 49. Duck Waddle.

Dog Gallop

Run on all fours, facing the floor, keep the seat up high and arms and legs straight.

Rabbit Jump

Squat down placing the hands on the ground the farthest distance possible in front of the feet. Jump the feet up to the hands. Move the hands out and jump to meet the hands again, performing a series of rabbit jumps.

Frog

Squat down placing the hands on the ground in between the knees. Pushing with the feet and hands at the same time, jump forward.

Rooster Hop

Hold the ankle of one foot with the hand on the same side of the body, hop on the opposite foot.

Kangaroo Hop

Place hands on the knees and jump.

Crab Walk

With the back facing the floor and with the hips lifted as high as possible, walk forward or backward on all fours (fig. 50).

Figure 50. Crab Walk.

Mule Kick

Bend forward placing the hands on the floor and kick feet into the air.

Worm Measure

From front leaning position (push-up) walk up outside the arms, then walk hands out in front to leaning position. Repeat.

Bicycle

Lying on the floor, support the back by placing the hands on the hips and the weight of the body on the shoulders. Imitate riding a bike by pedaling with the legs.

Criss Cross, Sit Stand

Sit down with the legs crossed. Try standing up while the arms are folded across the chest.

Thread the Needle

Fold the hands and then bring one leg up and through the arms of the folded hands and then the other; after this is accomplished, tuck one leg back through the hands and then the other to regain starting position.

Seal Walk

From a front leaning rest position, walk using arms only and drag the feet and legs (fig. 51).

Figure 51. Seal Walk.

Seal Slap

Place the hands on the floor in a front leaning rest position, push off hands, clap hands and assume front leaning rest position again.

Heel Click

From a standing position, jump into the air, click the heels together, and land without losing balance.

Human Rocker

Lie down on your stomach in prone position, hold your ankles with the hands and rock forward and backward on the stomach. Arch the back and keep the chin up.

Yoga Plough

Lie down in supine position with the arms placed out to the side, try to touch the floor behind the head with the feet.

Knee Walk

Assume a kneeling position, hold on to the ankles with the hands, and try to walk on the knees.

Up Spring

Assume a kneeling position and, by swinging the arms forward, come off the floor and jump into a stand.

Chorus Line Kick

In a standing position, kick upward one leg at a time, and try to touch an outstretched hand, which is at shoulder height.

Knee Dip

Holding the ankle of one leg with the hand on the same side

of the body, try to touch the knee to the floor by bending the other leg. Lean forward when performing this stunt.

Jump the Stick

Hold a plastic wand or hockey stick in front grasping each end of the stick with the hands. Try to jump up and through the arms, over the stick, and land without losing your balance.

Russian Dance

Assume a squat position and fold arms across the chest. Proceed to bounce and alternate kicking the legs out in front.

Partner Stunts

Seesaw

Partners hold hands facing each other. While one partner stands the other does a deep knee bend. Keeping a rhythm, take turns bending and standing.

Wheelbarrow

One child assumes a front leaning rest position while his partner grasps his knees and lifts them from the floor. The child in push-up position, walks forward on the hands while the partner holds his legs.

Lock-up

Two children seated back to back lock elbows and, by pushing off the floor with their feet simultaneously, stand up. It is easier to accomplish this task if the children are the same size (fig. 52).

Figure 52. Lock-up.

Get-up

Two children seated back to back perform the Siamese twins stunt with arms folded across their chest instead of having elbows locked.

Mirror

Two children stand facing one another as if they were looking into a mirror. One partner is the leader and makes a variety of movements the other child must imitate.

Leap Frog

First child bends at the waist, placing the hands on the knees, getting as low as possible. The second child places the hands on the partner's back and jumps over the partner. Switch places and progress forward.

Hoop Activities

Exploration

Children are asked to perform various tasks such as bending and stretching inside and outside of a hoop, making a bridge over the hoop, and balancing on different parts of their bodies inside the hoop. Children can make shapes inside the hoop when it is on the floor and while someone holds it in the air.

Hoops

Hoops are placed randomly on the floor and children perform a variety of locomotor activities (running, walking backward, skipping) or animal imitations (frogs, rabbits, snakes) outside of the hoops. When the instructor says the word *Hoop* the children must find and sit in a hoop as quickly as possible to wait for the next direction.

Hoop Balance

Children walk while attempting to balance hoops on their heads, fingers, thumbs, necks, and shoulders.

Locomotor Hoop

Children perform locomotor skills while holding the hoops waist height and standing inside them. Children perform such skills as galloping and running in different directions while listening for the instructor's command to *Freeze* at which time they must stop and listen for the next task to be given. The instructor may ask the children to use the hoop as if it were a steering wheel and they were driving a car. The hoops may also be tiny space capsules where children get in and blast off.

Falling Hoop

While standing inside the hoop, the child grasps the sides of the hoop and holds it directly over the head. On a signal by the instructor, the child drops the hoop, brings the arms quickly down by the side, and tries not to let the hoop touch the body.

Hoop Jumping

Since many children have difficulty turning the rope when first learning how to jump rope it can be advantageous to begin the learning of this skill using a hoop. Children grasp the hoop placing their hands one foot apart in front of them, while standing inside the hoop. By rotating the hands forward the children bring the hoop over the head so that it is in front of them. They can then step or jump into the hoop and repeat the action. Some children will be able to learn to jump the hoop backward or perform a double jump.

Hoop Roll

Children can pretend they are walking their pet hoops by rolling their hoops by their side backward, forward, and sideways with either hand. They may also practice rolling the hoops backward or forward and try to catch them before they fall. Also have them try to roll the hoop to a partner.

Hula

Children stand inside the hoop, holding it at waist level, with the hoop touching the back. The child must push the hoop with the hands sideways, at the same time swiveling the hips rhythmically to keep the momentum of the hoop going. If a child has difficulty, he can close his eyes and feel the hoop go down his body after the instructor gives the hoop an initial push.

Threading the Needle

The instructor rolls the hoop slowly as the child attempts to run through the hoop as it is moving. If the instructor is able to throw the hoop underhand with a backspin, it will be easier for the child to run through the hoop as it stays in one place for a brief moment before the return spin brings the hoop back to the instructor.

Hoop Circles

Children make the hoop turn in circles on their arms. The child lets the hoop rest on the wrist of an outstretched arm while the opposite hand grasps the hoop and pushes it downward. By moving the wrist up and down, the hoop will move in a circular pattern. If a child has difficulty performing the task, the instructor can aid by shaking hands with the child through the hoop and beginning the circular motion of the hoop for him.

Jump Rope Activities

Shapes and Letters

Children place the rope in different positions (bent, straight, coiled, curved), in a variety of shapes (circle, triangle, square), and in the shape of letters (C, P, L, S, V) and walk forward, backward, and sideways on the rope maintaining balance.

Snake

Instructor holds one end of a long rope and shakes it so that it wiggles on the ground. Children take turns or have contests competing against other children trying to catch the wiggly snake either by grasping the end of the rope with their hands or by stepping on it with their feet.

Stream

Two ropes are placed parallel to one another on the ground close together. Children jump over the two ropes, using either a standing broad jump or running long jump method. Every time a child is successful the ropes are moved farther apart enlarging the space between the ropes. Children learn how far they can jump.

High Water

Standing with the feet together, children jump over a rope that is held at a low height by two other children. Children who hold the rope raise it slightly after a child makes a successful jump and lower it if the rope is touched by a child. Children learn how high they can jump.

Limbo

Two children hold the ends of a rope and other children must go under the rope without touching the ground with anything but their feet. Children, who hold the rope, lower it after each successful attempt and raise the rope for those children who touch the rope or lose their balance. Children learn how low they can go.

Leap

Rope circles are placed on the floor in scatter formation or in a straight line and children must leap from one circle to another. Children can pretend they are frogs and the rope circles are lily pads that they must jump to.

Jump the Weight

A long rope weighted on one end with a bean bag is swung in a circular pattern by the instructor. Children standing in a half circle try to jump the rope as it is swung by the instructor.

Individual Jump Rope

Often the most difficult skill involved in jumping an individual rope for a beginner is turning the rope. The child should first practice turning the rope over the head from back to front, letting the rope land in front, and stepping over the rope. The child can work on swinging the rope over the head, letting it touch the ground, and jumping over it with two feet.

When the child can swing the rope smoothly, jumping over it continuously will be possible. The "jump rest" can be taught where the child takes a small rhythm jump between bigger jumps over the rope.

Long Jump Rope

In the beginning, the child should practice standing next to the rope and jump over it. The rope should then be swung slightly back and forth and the child can jump over it as the swinging arc is increased. It is advisable for the instructor to hold one of the ends of the rope, having the child who is jumping the rope face the instructor who can say *Jump* when it is necessary. Jumping when the rope is turned overhead is taught next, and the child should be reminded to jump in one place. The "jump rest," along with running in and out of a turned long rope, can be later learned.

Slice the Cheese

Two long ropes are held by two people who move the ropes in a slicing motion up and down. Children must try to go through the ropes without touching them.

Trampoline Activities

The trampoline consists of a metal frame holding a nylon bed attached by elastic shock cords. The ideal trampoline has a frame which is low to the ground and has a small bed size so that it is easy to spot performers, thus preventing injuries. Its size and weight make it easy to handle and to store. The trampoline is a safe piece of equipment if properly supervised and if safety is emphasized to the children. Children should bounce in the center of the bed and always get off the trampoline by sitting down on it and sliding off. When a child is bouncing on the bed, the instructor should use a safety belt or rope around the child's waist so that he can control the child's movement (fig. 53). Since bouncing can be tiring, the trampoline should be used only for short time periods.

Figure 53. Bouncing on the Trampoline.

Can you —

1. Bounce in a sitting position, a prone position, or a supine position?
2. Bounce standing up with feet shoulder width apart, flexing the knees, and jump the same time that the arms are swung upward?
3. Bounce ten times in a row?
4. Bounce and on a signal by the instructor stop bouncing

by performing a "kill bounce?" As the child starts to rise from the bed, he quickly lowers the body by flexing at the hips and knees so that the trunk does not rise.

5. Run in slow motion, in place, on the trampoline?
6. Bounce at different heights and body levels?
7. Clap your hands in front and in back while bouncing?
8. Perform jumping jacks while on the trampoline?
9. Perform a knee drop? As the child rises from the bed of the trampoline knees are flexed so that the lower legs are parallel to the bed and the back and hips are kept in a straight line. Land on the knees, shins, and instep, and swing the arms upward to return to a standing position.
10. Perform a seat drop? As you rise from the bed of the trampoline the legs are brought together, hips flexed, and legs lifted so that they are parallel to the trampoline bed. As you land, the hands push down on the bed and you rebound returning to a standing position.
11. Perform a hands and knees drop? As you perform a knee drop, the trunk is slowly curled forward and you land simultaneously on your hands and knees with the body parallel to the bed.
12. Perform a front drop? As you bounce upward the legs are raised backward and the trunk is lowered. In landing, the chest, the stomach, thighs, and hands touch the tramp at the same time.
13. Perform a combination? Perform a variety of moves in succession. Beginners can combine a seat drop with a knee drop or a knee drop with a seat drop.
14. Perform a turn? As you reach maximum bouncing height, twist in the air performing quarter, half, three-quarter, and full turns.
15. Bounce and play catch with a sponge ball at the same time?
16. Bounce to music keeping rhythm while bouncing and performing different drops?
17. Perform a routine? Combine knee, seat, and front drops with turns, claps, and jumping jacks to perform a routine of successive stunts.

Locomotor Games

Freeze

Children walk in any direction in the play area until the instructor says "freeze," at which time the children must stop and listen. Any participant who does not freeze on command must sit down for one turn, but is allowed to re-enter the game following the next command. All different types of locomotor skills, such as skipping, hopping, galloping, etc., may be used.

Bookends

One child is selected to be the leader and all the other children must find a partner and stand back to back with elbows linked. When the leader says "bookends" each player including the leader must find a new partner to link elbows with. The child who is left without a partner becomes the new leader and the game continues.

Fish and Whale

A child designated as the whale stands in the middle of the play area and the remaining children pretend to be fish standing at one end of the area (fig. 54). When the whale shouts "fish" the children try to run to the other side of the play area

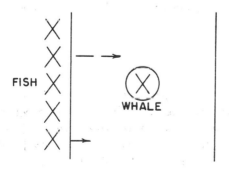

Figure 54. Fish and Whale.

without being tagged by the whale. If they are tagged, they must immediately sit down at the place where they were tagged. Those tagged become sitting whales and help to catch more fish. The last fish caught becomes the whale and the game continues.

Catch a Star

Bases, stars cut out of construction paper or rug samples, are scattered around the play area and called stars. Each child is positioned on a star except for one child who is designated as the moon. When the moon says "Stars are falling," all the players must change stars. The moon tries to claim a star vacated by a player. The child who does not secure a star becomes the moon for the next round. The game can be varied by having the children hop, skip, or crawl to a new star.

Switch

Children line up in two parallel lines facing one another on opposite sides of the playing area. Each player has a number corresponding to those players on the opposite line. One player is "it," and he stands in the middle of the playing area between the two lines of children. He calls out a number, and the two players that have that number try to exchange places by crossing the area. The player in the middle tries to tag one of them. If successful, he or she changes places with the child tagged.

Chase

Three children in a group of four hold hands. The fourth member attempts to tag a designated member of that group without reaching across hands that are held. In this group, player #1 will try to catch player #2 while #2 holds hands with players #3 and #4. Players #3 and #4 try to protect #2 by maneuvering themselves in front of player # 1 (fig. 55).

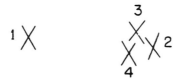

Figure 55. Chase.

Train Relay

Children are organized into teams in a relay formation (fig. 56). The first child in each line runs around a cone and returns to the line hooking up with the next person in line by putting his hands on his waist. They run the same route and hook up with the third person in line. The object of the game is to be the first line to finish with everyone hooked up and sitting down.

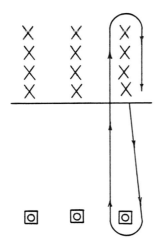

Figure 56. Train Relay.

Chapter 9

PHYSICAL FITNESS

Figure 57. Performing a Sit-up.

106

PHYSICAL fitness is an essential element in any motor development improvement program. A child's fitness level often dictates the intensity and duration with which he can participate in an activity. Normal play consisting of jumping, dodging, climbing, and racing provides adequate activity to develop fitness in most children. However, there are those children who because of environmental barriers, weight problems, sedentary lifestyles, and other reasons need a controlled physical fitness program.

Poor physical fitness can hamper a child's performance and slow down the rate of motor improvement. A child who has difficulty in hopping may demonstrate an adequate capacity to balance himself on one foot, but may be too weak to propel himself forward. Leg strengthening exercises should be incorporated into the child's total motor program to hasten remediation. Any child whose fitness limitations are restricting his motor development progress should work on strengthening those specific weak areas. If the child's overall physical fitness level is low, a daily exercise program incorporating flexibility exercise, progressive resistance exercise, and cardio-vascular training should be carried out.

Flexibility Exercise

Flexibility, the ability to move a joint in any direction, is a physical quality often neglected in physical development programs. Considerable flexibility is needed for successful performance in motor actions involved in daily activity and sports. Joint flexibility exercises should be done slowly, making sure that the joint is taken through its full range of motion. Each exercise should be repeated ten times.

Head Circles

The child rotates the head in a circular pattern.

Arm Circles

The child rotates the arms in a circular pattern clockwise and counterclockwise, starting with small circles and working towards large circles.

Shoulder Shrugs

Slowly, the child lifts his shoulders as if shrugging and then brings his shoulders downward as if someone is pulling his hands.

Side Stretches

The child puts his hands on his hips and bends sideways, forward, and backward in clockwise and counterclockwise directions.

Toe Touches

Slowly, the child bends down trying to touch his toes. Do not bounce.

Straddle Stretches

While sitting down with legs in a straddle position, the child stretches to try to touch the toes. This develops flexibility of the lower back and the hamstrings.

Hurdle Stretches

Sitting in a hurdling position, the child stretches forward to touch the front foot. Switch the forward leg. This develops flexibility of the quadraceps and hamstrings.

Leg Circles

In a standing position, the child moves a leg in a circular pattern. Alternate legs when performing this.

Progressive Resistance Exercise

A child who demonstrates muscular weakness should perform a series of progressive resistance exercises daily. The following exercises are recommended for children who want to improve their strength in a certain area or gain an overall strength increase. It is beneficial if a physical education teacher can share with the child or his parents the exercises that will be the most advantageous for the student's individual fitness needs in accordance with exercise equipment availability. It is important to remember that children who are low in physical fitness need to have success-oriented experiences for personal motivation. It is generally better to start the child's strength improvement program with simple exercises involving a lot of repetitions, than working too early to develop maximum strength production. Children can see steady improvement, increasing the chance for long-term progress in their performance. These exercises should be done twice a day within a close time span.

Curls for Arm Strength

Using any type of 1- or 2-pound weights (weighted juice cans) the child places the weight in the hand and flexes at the elbows. The child can perform the exercise for a number of repetitions. This develops the biceps.

Push-ups for Arm and Shoulder Strength

The child lies in a prone position on the floor with his hands shoulders width apart, and he pushes off with the hands. The body is lifted with only the toes and hands on the floor. At first, push-ups can be performed by simply lowering the body to the floor. The child can progress by performing push-ups with the knees touching the floor, to raising and lowering the entire body from toes and hands. This develops the triceps, anterior deltoids, pectoralis major clavicula, and serratus anterior muscles.

Military Press for Arm and Shoulder Strength

The child stands, holding 1- or 2-pound weights in the hands and pushes the weights above the head into the air a number of times. This develops the triceps, anterior deltoids, pectoralis major clavicula, and serratus anterior muscles.

Pull-ups for Arm and Shoulder Strength

The child hangs from a stationary bar by the hands with his arms fully extended and he flexes at the elbow until his chin is above the bar. If the child has difficulty, the instructor can help by grasping the child's waist and aiding him through the exercise. This develops the biceps, pectoralis major sternal, latissimus dorsi, and teres major muscles.

Bench Press for Arm and Shoulder Strength

While lying on his back, the child pushes one to five pound weights into the air a number of times. Weights should be pressed into the air directly above the shoulders. This develops the triceps, anterior deltoids, pectoralis major clavicula, and serratus anterior muscles.

Modified Dips for Arm and Shoulder Strength

The child sits on the floor with his back against a bench that is approximately 18 inches high. He bends his elbows and places the palm of the hands on the bench. The exercise is done by extending the elbows, pushing off the bench, and lifting the body off the floor so that only the feet are touching. This develops the triceps, anterior deltoids, pectoralis major clavicula, rhomboid, and trapezius muscles.

Lateral Arm Raises for Shoulder and Upper Back Strength

The child is in a standing position and holds a one or two pound weight in the hands, keeping the elbows extended, and raises the arms sideways and upward. This develops the middle deltoids, supraspinatus, serratus anterior, and trapezius muscles.

Supine Arm Raises for Chest Strength

While lying on his back with arms extended at shoulder height, the child uses the weights in his hands and raises his arms over his chest. This develops pectoralis major and minor, serratus anterior, and anterior deltoid muscles.

Sit-ups for Abdominal Strength

Sit-ups should be performed with the knees in a flexed position. If the child is unable to perform a sit-up with his hands behind his head, he may use his arms to throw his weight forward. Twenty sit-ups at one time is sufficient. Instead of doing more sit-ups, the sit-up can be made more difficult by raising the legs or lying on an incline with the head lower than the feet. The child can perform a V-sit, bringing the arms and legs up together. This develops the rectus abdominus, external and internal obliques, psoas, iliacus, pectineus, and rectus femoris.

Knee Extensions for Leg Strength

The child puts on heavy shoes, boots, or light ankle weights and, while sitting in a chair, extends the knee and raises the foot. This develops the quadraceps femoris.

Knee Flexions for Leg Strength

The child lies on his stomach with heavy shoes, boots, or light ankle weights on and flexes at the knee raising the foot. This develops the hamstrings.

Jumps for Leg Strength

The child jumps in place for a time limit and tries to increase the time each workout. The child can also jump from one designated starting point to a finish point, counting the number of jumps it takes to get there. The child can work towards decreasing the number of traveling jumps by taking longer jumps. This develops the hamstrings and the quadriceps femoris.

Endurance

Each child in a fitness program should be encouraged to perform some cardio-vascular exercise daily that will increase his heart rate for a sufficient period of time. A variety of training techniques should be explored to find which is the most suitable and enjoyable. The exercise or activity may change often in order to make the training interesting.

Distance Running

One very effective method of improving a child's cardio-vascular strength is by having the child run a short distance and increase that distance gradually. A running chart can be designed so that the child earns credit for the running distance he completes (see Appendix C). Every time the child runs 300 yards, he colors in a box. Six boxes would equal a mile. Incentives can be set up such as a reward for the accumulation of a designated mileage.

Another running method used to improve endurance is to have the child jog a certain distance each time, and decrease the amount of time it takes to cover the distance each time out. It may be beneficial to have a group of children train in this method as the added impetus of other children racing will generally inspire the child to run harder. If a group is running, the children should be reminded that they are running to improve their individual time and try to realize that they all have the same goal of time improvement and not simply being faster than their fellow runners.

Jumping Rope

Rope jumping is another means of increasing the heart rate, and a limited amount of space is needed. Charts can be designed that are similar to those used for distance running in order to motivate the child. Music to accompany the jumping helps in developing a consistent rhythm and makes jumping more enjoyable.

Aerobic Dance

Children can learn a series of simple dance exercises that can be performed to music. A workout of this type couples flexibility and strength exercise with endurance. It is an extremely beneficial activity that should be directed by an instructor.

Sports

Children who are skilled in a particular sport or activity may wish to engage in that activity for a certain amount of time each day. Sports such as soccer and swimming provide ample training, if done on a daily basis.

APPENDICES

ANDOVER PERCEPTUAL MOTOR TEST

1. Static Balance

Description:
Student is asked to stand on one foot for six seconds with the other foot six inches off the ground and beside the opposite leg, arms folded across chest, and eyes closed.
Rules:
Maximum number tested at one time should be three.
  Scoring:
  3 can perform task with arms folded, eyes closed.
  2 can perform task with arms by sides eyes open.
  1 cannot balance for 6 seconds.

2. Dynamic Balance

Equipment:
One primary balance beam that is approximately five feet long and six inches high.
Description:
Student is asked to walk the length of a primary beam.
Rules:
Maximum number tested at one time should be one. The walk should be done slowly with one foot placed directly in front of the other.
  Scoring:
  3 can walk the length with control and without stepping off.
  2 step off once, but seems to have control.
  1 cannot cross the beam without difficulty.

3. Eye-hand Coordination

Equipment:
One or two 8-inch balls.

117

Description:
Student is asked to dribble an 8-inch ball a consecutive number of times.
Age four — 3 two-hand drop-catches.
Age five — 3 two-hand drop-catches or 3 dribbles.
Age six — 6 dribbles.
Age seven — 8 dribbles.
Rules:
Maximum number tested should be one for kindergarten (age five) and two for grade 1. If, on the first bounce only, the child's ball inadvertently hits a body part and rolls away, the child may have a second trial.
  Scoring:
  3 completes the task without difficulty
  2 has some difficulty
    a. uses a slapping motion
    b. cannot dribble below shoulder height.
    c. the child manages to complete the required dribbles, but the ball does not contact the floor within the same relative space each time.
  1 cannot dribble the ball in his space the required number of times.

4. Locomotion—Crawl

Description:
Student is asked to crawl approximately 10 feet.
Rules:
Maximum number of students tested at one time should be four. Teacher should emphasize that the crawl be done *slowly*. Teacher should be watching for cross patterning, crawling with right arm forward and left knee forward and alternating left arm forward and right knee forward.
  Scoring:
  3 completes task without difficulty (cross-pattern).
  2 has some difficulty.
    a. may start with left arm and left leg forward but then corrects to proper cross-pattern.
    b. may interchange correct cross-patterning then bilateral

motion, then correct cross-patterning, etc.
1 cannot perform task.
   a. crawls right arm, right leg or left arm left leg sequence.
   b. exhibits no definite technique and does not use the legs in the motion.

5. *Locomotion—Jump Backward*

Description:
Student stands with heels touching the front edge of a 2-inch line on the floor and is asked to jump backwards one time over the line so that his toes "clear" the line (fig. 53).

Figure 58. Locomotion — Jump Backward.

Rules:
Maximum number tested at one time should be two. According to teacher discretion, if the child exhibits difficulty due to lack of attention in listening or misunderstanding, the teacher should allow a second trial that immediately follows the first attempt.
  Scoring:
  3 completes task without difficulty.
  2 has some difficulty.
    a. upon landing one foot is touching line slightly.

b. slight movement of one foot on landing.
1 cannot propel himself/herself backward.
  a. both feet land squarely on line.
  b. great deal of movement of feet on landing.
  c. falls down.

6A. Locomotion—Hopping on Left Foot

Description:
Student is asked to hop on his left foot a distance of 10 feet.
Rules:
Maximum number tested at one time should be one.
  Scoring:
  3 completes task without difficulty.
  2 has some difficulty.
    a. toe or foot touches floor once.
  1 cannot hop on the left foot.
    a. loses balance and falls.
    b. toe and/or foot touches floor more than once.

6B. Locomotion—Hopping on Right Foot

Description, Rules, and Scoring:
Same as 6A, but with opposite leg.

7. Spatial Awareness

Equipment:
One dowel or stick.
Description:
Student is asked to step over a stick held knee high, then walk under stick held shoulder high, and then go between a stick and the wall while the stick is held vertically 10 inches from the wall.
Rules:
Maximum number tested at one time should be one. Student cannot crawl or creep under the stick, he must bend and walk under.
  Scoring:

3 completes all tasks without touching the stick.
2 students touch part of the body to either stick or wall in one of the tasks.
1 student touches either stick or wall in two or three of the tasks.

8. *Rhythm*

Description:
Student is asked to repeat an "even" three-beat clapping pattern and an "uneven" three-beat clapping pattern that is presented by the teacher one at a time. Teacher claps, then student claps.

Rules:
Maximum number tested at one time is one. Make certain that there are as few distractions as possible when testing, especially auditory distractions, since they interfere with the student's hearing of the correct pattern.

3 EVEN	clap	clap		clap
	x	x		x
3 UNEVEN	clap	pause	clap	clap
	x		x	x
	OR			
	clap	clap	pause	clap
	x	x		x

Scoring:
3 completes both patterns without difficulty.
2 is able to complete only one pattern successfully.
1 is unable to complete either pattern.

MOTOR SKILLS ASSESSMENT SHEETS

MOTOR SKILLS AGE FIVE, SIX, SEVEN

Skills Accomplished:

Name _____

Skills to be Attained:
Student will be able —

	Trial Assessment		Evaluation	
	Some difficulty	Satisfactory	Some difficulty	Satisfactory
MOTOR SKILLS AGE FIVE				
to identify different body parts and know their use in movement				
to crawl in a cross pattern a distance of 10 feet				
to walk at a consistent gait, at varying speeds, with arms and legs in opposition				
to run in a coordinated manner, a distance of 30 yards, with integration of arms and legs				
to make appropriate spatial judgements when moving over, under, and between objects and obstacles				
to move in the space of the gymnasium without contact with other students and objects				
to move in one's personal space in the gymnasium with controlled body movements				
to climb steps, jungle gym, and vertical ladder with a cross pattern motion				
to jump forward and backward over a line, maintaining balance				
to hop on the right foot and then the left a distance of 15 ft.				

Name _____

Skills to be Attained:

Student will be able —

	Trial Assessment		Evaluation	
	Some difficulty	Satisfactory	Some difficulty	Satisfactory
to balance on one foot for six seconds	—	—	—	—
to walk the length of a 4-inch wide balance beam	—	—	—	—
to throw an 8-inch playground ball at a wall that is 15 feet away	—	—	—	—
to dribble an 8-inch playground ball three consecutive times	—	—	—	—
to catch an 8-inch sponge ball thrown from a distance of 5 feet	—	—	—	—
to catch an 8-inch playground ball from a bounce	—	—	—	—
to kick an 8-inch playground ball at a wall which is a distance of 10 feet away	—	—	—	—
to clap in short rhythmic patterns	—	—	—	—

MOTOR SKILLS AGE SIX

	Trial Assessment		Evaluation	
	Some difficulty	Satisfactory	Some difficulty	Satisfactory
to distinguish between the left and right sides of his own body	—	—	—	—
to run on the balls of the feet, with feet pointing forward, a distance of 30 yards using the proper arm-leg opposition	—	—	—	—
to jump over a line forward, backward, and sideways while maintaining balance	—	—	—	—
to jump across the gymnasium with the knees bent, taking off and landing with two feet	—	—	—	—

Name _____
Skills to be Attained:
Student will be able —

Skills Accomplished:

Skill	Trial Assessment		Evaluation	
	Some difficulty	Satisfactory	Some difficulty	Satisfactory
to hop on the right foot then the left a distance of 20 feet	—	—	—	—
to gallop, keeping one foot ahead of the other, a distance of 20 yards	—	—	—	—
to skip, by taking a series of step-hops, a distance of 20 yards	—	—	—	—
to jump ten times on the trainer trampoline with good body control	—	—	—	—
to walk forward on the rungs and sides of the length of a horizontal ladder	—	—	—	—
to ride a scooter a distance of 30 feet while maintaining balance	—	—	—	—
to hit a round balloon with the hand into the air five times	—	—	—	—
to throw an 8-inch playground ball a distance of 10 feet	—	—	—	—
to catch an 8-inch playground ball from a bounce thrown from 10 feet	—	—	—	—
to dribble an 8-inch playground ball six consecutive times	—	—	—	—
to kick an 8-inch playground ball a distance of 20 feet	—	—	—	—
to tie his/her own shoe laces	—	—	—	—
to know basic games and activities for his/her age group	—	—	—	—

Skills Accomplished:

	Trial Assessment		Evaluation	
	Some difficulty	Satisfactory	Some difficulty	Satisfactory

Name _____
Skills to be Attained:
Student will be able —

MOTOR SKILLS AGE SEVEN

— to determine the right and left directions in space in relation to his own body

— to run in a coordinated manner, with the ability to change direction when an obstacle is encountered

— to jump off a height of 26 inches and land with feet together and maintain balance

— to gallop a distance of 20 yards with the right foot and then the left foot as the lead

— to skip, taking a minimum amount of steps, 20 yards

— to perform a forward roll on a tumbling mat

— to balance on one foot with arms folded across chest for 6 seconds

— to walk forward, backward, and sideways the length of a low, 4 inch wide balance beam

— to perform a knee drop and seat drop while bouncing on a trainor trampoline

— to ride a bicycle unassisted a distance of 30 yards

— to hit a round balloon with a paddle five times into the air

Name _____

Skills to be Attained:

Student will be able —

Skills Accomplished:

	Trial Assessment		Evaluation	
	Some difficulty	Satisfactory	Some difficulty	Satisfactory
___ to throw an 8-inch playground ball to a partner 6 feet away				
___ to throw a 5-inch playground ball at a wall 10 feet away, using an overhand throw				
___ to catch an 8-inch playground ball in the air while in motion				
___ to dribble an 8-inch playground ball while walking a distance of 20 feet				
___ to know basic games and activities for his/her age group				

SAMPLE CHARTS AND AWARDS

TWENTY-FIVE MILE RUN

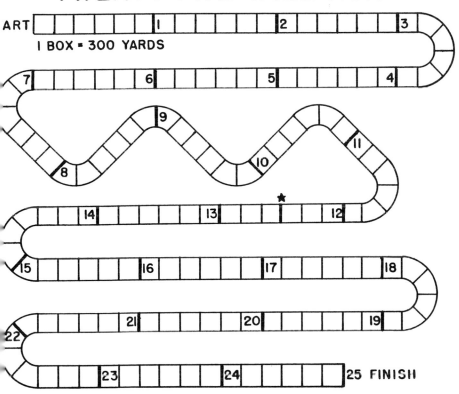

I BOX = 300 YARDS

THIS IS TO CERTIFY THAT

RAN THE ACCUMULATED DISTANCE OF 12.6 MILES OR THE
EQUIVALENCY OF THE DISTANCE FROM ANDOVER, MASSACHUSETTS
TO CANOBIE LAKE, NEW HAMPSHIRE.

PHYSICAL EDUCATION TEACHER   PHYSICAL EDUCATION TEACHER

I TRY HARD AWARD

_____

MOST IMPROVED AWARD

_____

HARDEST WORKER AWARD

_____

THIS IS TO CERTIFY THAT

_____

RAN THE ACCUMULATED DISTANCE OF___MILES, DURING THE SCHOOL YEAR OF _____ .

_____   _____
PHYSICAL EDUCATION TEACHER   **SCHOOL PRINCIPAL**

BIBLIOGRAPHY

American Association for Health, Physical Education and Recreation: *Physical Activities for the Mentally Retarded (Ideas for Instruction).* Washington, D.C., 1968.

Braley, William T. Konicki, Geraldine, and Leedy, Catherine: *Daily Sensorimotor Training Activities: A Handbook for Teachers and Parents of Preschool Children.* Freeport, Ed Activities, 1968.

Capon, Jack: *Perceptual Motor Development.* Belmont, California, Fearon, 1975.

Corbin, Charles B.: *Becoming Physically Educated in the Elementary Schools.* Philadelphia, Lea & Febiger, 1969.

Cratty, Bryant J.: *Developmental Sequences of Perceptual-Motor Tasks: Movement Activities for Neurologically Handicapped and Retarded Children and Youth.* Mt. Prospect, Illinois, Activity Rec, 1967.

Croke, Katherine Bissell, and Fairchild, Betty Jacinto: *Let's Play Games!* National Easter Seal Society for Crippled Children and Adults, 1978.

Fleuegelman, Anore W. (Ed.): *The New Games Book.* Garden City, New York, Doubleday, 1976.

Kirchner, Glenn: *Physical Education for Elementary School Children,* 3rd ed. Dubuque, Iowa, Wm C Brown, 1974.

Miller, Arthur G., Cheffers, John T. F., and Whitcomb, Virginia: *Physical Education Teaching Human Movement in the Elementary Schools,* 4th ed. Englewood Cliffs, New Jersey, P-H, 1974.

Mosston, Muska: *Developmental Movement.* Columbus, Ohio, Merrill, 1965.

Mourouzis, Ann, Wemble, Donna, Wheeler, James, Williams, Linda, and Zurcher, Susan: *Body Management Activities: A Guide to Perceptual-Motor Training.* Dayton, Ohio, MWZ Associates, 1970.

Orlick, Terry: *The Cooperative Sports and Games Book, Challenge Without Competition.* New York, Pantheon, 1978.

INDEX